AF361402

The Sacred Congregation for the
Propagation of the Faith

This dissertation was approved by the Reverend Frederick R. McManus, J.C.D., as director, and by Professor Stephan G. Kuttner, J.U.D., S.J.D., J.C.D., LL.D., and the Reverend Bernard F. Deutsch, J.C.D., I.C.D., as readers.

THE CATHOLIC UNIVERSITY OF AMERICA
CANON LAW STUDIES
No. 420

The Sacred Congregation for the Propagation of the Faith

A DISSERTATION

*Submitted to the Faculty of the School of Canon Law
of The Catholic University of America in Partial
Fulfillment of the Requirements for the
Degree of Doctor of Canon Law*

BY

RAPHAEL H. SONG, M.A., J.C.L.
Priest of the Vicariate Apostolic of Taegu, Korea

THE CATHOLIC UNIVERSITY OF AMERICA PRESS
WASHINGTON, D. C.
1961

Nihil Obstat:

FREDERICK R. McMANUS, J.C.D.
Censor Deputatus

Washington, D. C., July 5, 1961

Imprimatur:

✠ JOHN B. SYE, D.D.
*Episcopus Tit. Chomatitanus nec non
Vicarius Apostolicus Taeguensis*

Taegu, Korea, July 12, 1961

Printed by
THE WICKERSHAM PRINTING COMPANY
Lancaster, Pennsylvania

DEDICATED TO
THE BELOVED MEMORY OF
MY FATHER AND MOTHER

FOREWORD

Since there was no body corresponding to the Congregation for
the Propagation of the Faith in the early or medieval history of
the Roman Curia, from the end of the first century until the
Second Council of the Lateran in 1139, mission law was embodied
in letters of the Roman Pontiffs and in decisions of the ten ecumenical councils held between 325 and 1139. Practically speak-
ing, there was no such thing as mission law in any strict sense
until the mission faculties were given in the XIIth and XIIIth
centuries. Before this time, mission law coincided with the common law of the Church.

On June 22, 1622, Gregory XV officially established the Congregation for the Propagation of the Faith by the constitution
Inscrutabili. It soon surpassed all the other Congregations by
the extraordinary extent of its powers and jurisdiction. It re-
sembled the other Congregations in organization, but it differed
entirely from them in the range of its authority. From the beginning of its existence, the two distinct purposes of the Congregation were to reconquer by spiritual arms, by prayers and
good works, by preaching and catechising, the countries that had
been lost to the Church in the debacle of the XVIth century;
and to organize into an efficient corps the numerous missionary
enterprises for the diffusion of the Gospel in heathen lands.

On June 29, 1908, Pius X issued the constitution *Sapienti consilio*, and on September 29, 1908, two subsidiary documents were
published. Through these acts there was effected a complete
juridical reorganization of the Roman Curia. The two chief
aims of the curial reorganization were to establish the uniformity of the Congregations arranged by Sixtus V in the constitution
Immensa of January 22, 1588, and to determine clearly the competence of the respective Congregations so as to adapt the effective administrative organization of the central authorities to
requirements and problems. The endeavor of Pius X circum-

scribed accurately the territorial, personal, and material competence of the Congregation for the Propagation of the Faith.

The purpose of this dissertation is to trace the historical development of the Congregation for the Propagation of the Faith and to examine its constitution and the limits of its competence.

The writer is deeply grateful to His Excellency, the Most Reverend John B. Sye, D.D., Titular Bishop of Choma and Vicar Apostolic of Taegu, Korea, for the opportunity to undertake graduate studies in Canon Law. He also chooses this occasion to express his sincere gratitude to the members of the Faculty of the School of Canon Law of The Catholic University of America for their devoted assistance and to all who helped in the preparation of this work.

TABLE OF CONTENTS

CHAPTER V

CHAPTER VI

CHAPTER I

HISTORICAL BACKGROUND OF THE CONGREGATION

Article 1. Origin of the Roman Congregations in General

At first the Roman Curia was merely the assembly of the Roman clerics, priests, and deacons who, together with the Bishop of Rome, deliberated on the common affairs of the Church.[1] For more difficult matters, however, when great knowledge, wisdom, and authority were required, neighboring bishops were frequently called upon for the final decision of controversies.[2] Such an assembly was named the *presbyterium,* or synod, or Roman council.[3]

In the XIth century, the *consistorium* was gradually substituted for the *presbyterium.* This *consistorium* was a meeting of the cardinals in the presence of the Roman Pontiff together with the *auditorium Papae,* which came into existence at the time of Alexander III (1159-1181). This *auditorium* was formed by prelates other than cardinals, whose office was to judge contentious and criminal cases. The *auditorium* was the precursor of the Roman Rota.[4] The final demise of the *presbyterium* occurred during the pontificate of Innocent III (1198-1216).[5]

With the establishment of the Congregation of the Inquisition in 1542, a more stable and organized system of congregations

---

[1] Stanghetti, *Prassi della S.C. de Propaganda Fide* (Romae: Officium Libri Catholici, 1943), p. 13 (hereafter referred to as *Prassi*).

[2] Monin, *De Curia Romana* (Lovanii, 1912), p. 4.

[3] Stanghetti, *Prassi,* p. 13.

[4] *Loc. cit.*

[5] Hilling, *Procedure at the Roman Curia* (New York, 1907), p. 13. Cf. De Luca, *Relatio Romanae Curiae Forensis,* in suo magno opere *Theatrum Veritatis et Iustitiae* (16 toms. in 9, Coloniae, 1706), Tom. VII, lib. 15, pt. 2, discursus IV, n. 6; Maroto, *Institutiones Iuris Canonici ad Normam Novi Codicis* (2 vols., Vol. I, 3. ed., Romae, 1919-1921), Vol. II, n. 826 (hereafter referred to as *Institutiones*).

1

appeared for the first time under Paul III (1534-1549).[6] Later, the various departments of the Roman Curia were formed in their present structure under Sixtus V (1585-1590),[7] who established a curia of fifteen Congregations.[8]

On June 29, 1908, Pius X reformed the Roman Curia thoroughly,[9] and his important reform was substantially incorporated into the Code of Canon Law in 1918, although even then a few additional changes were made in the Curia. There are now eleven Congregations,[10] three Tribunals,[11] and five Offices:[12]

1. Holy Office
2. Consistorial Congregation
3. Congregation for the Discipline of the Sacraments
4. Congregation of the Council
5. Congregation for Religious
6. Congregation for the Propagation of the Faith
7. Congregation for Sacred Rites
8. Ceremonial Congregation
9. Congregation for Extraordinary Ecclesiastical Affairs
10. Congregation for Seminaries and Universities
11. Congregation for the Oriental Church

---

1. Sacred Penitentiary

[6] De Luca, *Relatio Romanae Curiae Forensis*, discursus XIV, n. 6; Monin, *op. cit.*, p. 9; Capello, *De Romana Curia* (2 vols., Romae, 1911-1912), I, 59.

[7] Stanghetti, *Prassi*, p. 13.

[8] *Bullarum Diplomatum et Privilegiorum Sanctorum Romanorum Pontificum Taurinensis Editio* (24 vols. and appendix, Augustae Taurinorum, 1857-1872), VIII, 985-997 (hereafter referred to as *Bull. Rom.*); Niccolo del Re, *La Curia Romana* (2 vols., Romae, Edizioni di Storia e Letteratura, 1952), pp. 19-21.

[9] Pius X, const. *Sapienti consilio*, 29 iun. 1908—*Acta Apostolicae Sedis*, Commentarium Officiale (Romae, 1909-), I (1909), 7-9 (hereafter cited as *AAS*); *Codicis Iuris Canonici Fontes cura Ēmi Pietri Card. Gasparri editi* (9 vols., Romae, 1923-1939), n. 682 (hereafter cited as *Fontes*).

[10] Can. 247-257.

[11] Can. 258-259; 1598-1605.

[12] Can. 260-264.

2. Roman Rota
3. Apostolic Signatura

---

1. Apostolic Chancery
2. Apostolic Datary
3. Apostolic Camera
4. Secretariate of State
5. Secretariate of Briefs to Princes and of Latin Letters

ARTICLE 2. COMMISSION UNDER PIUS V

Throughout the XVth and XVIth centuries, the Church still fostered the missionary activities of the Franciscans and Dominicans. While throughout Christendom the Church was suffering great losses, it was also acquiring new territories in remote regions. The discoveries made by the Spaniards and Portuguese, both in the East and in the West, awakened great apostolic zeal among religious of all orders particularly among the Jesuits and Capuchins.[13]

At this time, an internal reform of head and members of the Church as a fundamental prerequisite for the missionary work and the purging of undeniable defects and obstacles to the entire work of the propagation of the faith was necessary.[14] With the Counter Reformation and the religious revival of the period, it was above all the papal Curia which, after Alexander VI's Bull of Demarcation (May 4, 1493), manifested an increased cooperation with missionary work.

From this time on the Curia devoted a still more active attention and support to the pagan apostolate. Alexander VI's immediate successor, Paul III (1534-1549), showed a keen interest in missionary needs. He protected missionary progress, nominated many missionary bishops, and shared in the development of the missions of the Society of Jesus, although he was not the first pope to introduce serious ecclesiastical reforms nor the earliest

---

[13] Funk, *History of the Church* (2 vols., London: Burnes Oates, 1931), II, 158; Schmidlin, *Catholic Mission History*, trans. by Matthias Braun (Techny, Ill.: Mission Press, 1933), p. 255.

[14] Schmidlin, *loc. cit.*

representative of the new missionary outlook and method of central organization of the missions. The first definite missionary organization was established in the time of Pius V (1566-1572).[15]

A question may arise concerning the first founder of a central mission organization. The celebrated circular letter of the cardinals who had been placed by Gregory XV at the head of the reestablished missionary movement during the first half of the XVIIth century would seem to indicate that the initial idea of a central mission organization originated with Pius IV (1559-1565) and his zealous co-operator in the direction of ecclesiastical affairs, Cardinal Nepote Carlo Borromeo.[16] This statement, however, must be questioned. Pius IV, who approved the reform activities of the Council of Trent, was certainly most deeply interested in the missions, but he was preoccupied with putting into effect the decrees of the Council and was overtaken by death after only six years of his pontificate, when the program had not yet been completely accomplished. Pius IV had, therefore, neither time nor opportunity to consider the serious problem of the central organization of mission work or of the emancipation of the missions from civil control.[17]

Certainly, missionary work among the pagans was not neglected by Pius IV. A letter in Latin believed to have been written to him during the early months of 1565 by Quinto Mario Corrado indicates the missionary concern of this Pope. Pius IV had directed Cardinal Sirleto to gather a group of some twenty persons to help the apostolic missions by translating into Latin the reports which were written and submitted by the missionaries of the Society of Jesus in the East Indies: *"ut, quos ii labores pro Christi nomine adhuc susceptos habent, non modo intra Italiae aut Hispaniae fines legerentur, sed ubicumque ad illorum exempla sese pro religione devovendi quamplurimos accendere*

---

[15] Streit, "Missionsgedanke in seiner neuzeitlichen Entwicklung," *Zeitschrift für Missionswissenschaft* (Münster, 1917), VII, 5; Schmidlin, *op. cit.*, p. 257.

[16] Castelucci, "Il risveglio dell'attivita missionaria e le prime origini della S.C. de Propaganda Fide," *Le Conferenze al Laterno* (Roma, 1924), p. 138.

[17] Castelucci, *loc. cit.*

intersit." Some eminent Latinists of the time such as Lolli, Manuzio, Sigonio, Ferrari, and Poggiano were invited to co-operate.[18]

The first Pope to erect a stable commission to care for the general and permanent organization of the missions was not Pius IV, but his immediate successor, Pius V (1566-1572), a Dominican.[19]

With the new resurgence of Christianity in the XVIth and XVIIth centuries, a grave problem arose between Pius V and Philip II of Spain. The Pope tried to restore religious matters to the control of the Church and to remove them from the authority of the King. Pius V felt strongly about the abuse of ecclesiastical functions by Philip's ministers. From his point of view, Philip complained that the Pope did not have sufficient authority to control the Spanish Inquisition which had been instituted independently of the Holy See.[20]

Because of these controversies, Pius V organized a special mission department in the Roman Curia in order to provide a more systematic organization of missionary endeavor and to maintain the work of the world-mission on a more uniform basis. The specific purpose was to counterbalance the growing invasion of the Spanish Council of the Indies and to eliminate abuses of any kind which were coming from that Council.[21]

In April of 1568, through the Apostolic Nuncio, Giambattista Castagna, Pius V had expressed his intention to Philip II of sending to the West Indies a person with the authority of an Apostolic Nuncio directly under the Holy See, *"una persona che*

[18] Castelucci, "art. cit.," p. 139, footnote n. 1: "Lagomarsini, *Julii Pogiani sunensis epistolae et orationes olim collectae ab Antonio Maria Gratiano* (Roma, 1758), p. 69: 'non multo post idem Cardinalis (Sirleto) ex mandato Pii IV commisit, ut nonnullas epistolas de Indorum rebus in latinum sermonem transferret.'"

[19] Castelucci, *Il risveglio*, p. 140.

[20] Walsh, *Philip II* (London–New York: Sheed & Ward, 1937), pp. 500-502; Funk, *op. cit.*, p. 151.

[21] Bertini, "S.C. di Propaganda Fide," *Enciclopedia Cattolica* (12 vols., Città del Vaticano, 1948-1954), IV, 330.

dipendesse immediatamente da [la] *Santa Sede, e con autorità di Nuncio.*" [22]

Philip II rejected the intention of Pius V, and as a result of the rejection, the definite idea of establishing a Congregation for the Propagation of the Faith came to Pius V. His purpose, then, was to free missionary activities from political interference and from the material interest and the nationalistic tendencies of Philip II.[23]

A few months before the organization of two separate commissions which Pius V planned, one for the conversion of pagans and the other for the care of heretics, an important suggestion was made to the Pope by the Jesuit General, Francis Borgia, and the secretary of the General, Polanco. Moreover, on May 20, 1568, the General visited the Pope, in the company of the Portuguese Ambassador, Aivaro Castro, and obtained a definite sanction from the Pope for the institution of a commission for the conversion of the infidels.[24]

Cardinal Antonio Carafa states in the consistorial diary that, while the consistory was being held on July 23, 1568, Pius V privately ordered some cardinals of different nations to organize a commission for the purpose of the conversion of heretics in Northern Europe. The Cardinals of the commission were Ottone (Truchsess) from Augsburg (residing, then, in the Curia), Filiberto Naldo (Babou) from Bourdaisière (French), Antonio Perrenot (Granvelle), from Borgogna, and Gianfrancesco Commendone from Venice.[25] Pius V also ordered some other cardinals to institute a second commission which would provide for the

---

[22] Pastor, *The History of the Popes* (34 vols., Vols. I-VI edited by Frederick Ignatius Antrobus; Vols. VII-XXIV by Ralph Francis Kerr; Vols. XXV-XXXIV by Dom Ernest Graf, St. Louis: B. Herder, 1898-1941), XVIII, 1-6.

[23] Castelucci, *Il risveglio*, p. 145; Bertini, "art. cit.," XII, 330; Schmidlin, "Die Gründung der Propagandakongregation," *Zeitschrift für Missionswissenschaft* (Münster, 1922), XII, 1-14.

[24] Polanco, *Monumenta Historica Societatis Iesu* (2 vols., Madrid, 1917), II, 688.

[25] Castelucci, "art. cit.," pp. 145-146.

development of the Church in the East and West Indies. The Cardinals were Marcantonio Amulio, Alessandro Crivelli, Guglielmo Sirleto, and Antonio Carafa.[26]

The information given by Polanco is found in a letter of Francis Borgia who on August 2, 1568, wrote Gerolamo Nadal concerning the establishment of the two commissions by Pius V.[27]

As Francis Borgia notes, the second commission began to meet immediately, but the activity of the first commission is not known to us. It is difficult to say whether it ever met or whether its activity was so small as not to be noticed.[28] Concerning the activities of the second commission, there is abundant documentation in the letters of Cardinal Alessandrino to the Nuncio of Spain, Giambattista Castagna, and to Cardinal Amulio, who was the Prefect of the commission.[29]

On August 19, 1568, Cardinal Nepote Michele Bonelli, commonly called Cardinal Alessandrino, informed the Apostolic Nuncio Castagna of an instruction issued by the commission. This included six Apostolic briefs, dated August 17 and 18. The briefs were addressed to Philip II, to Cardinal Spinoza (the President of the Spanish Council of the Indies), to the members of the Spanish Council of the Indies, to Francis of Toledo (Governor of Perù), to Peter Menéndez (Governor of Florida), and to Martin Enriquez (Governor of Mexico).[30] At the same time Cardinal Alessandrino notified the Nuncio, Giambattista Castagna, that all spiritual matters concerning the conversion of the pagans should be communicated to the newly erected commission. Finally, on the same day, Cardinal Amulio also notified the Nuncio that he should assure everyone concerning the intentions of the Holy Father; Pius V had decided to make the changes because of his pastoral duty to restore full authority

[26] *Collectanea Sacrae Congregationis de Propaganda Fide* (2 vols., Romae, 1907), I, n. 2 (hereafter referred to as *Coll. S.C.P.F.*).

[27] Castelucci, "art. cit.," p. 147.

[28] *Ibid.*, p. 148.

[29] *Loc. cit.*

[30] Castelucci, "art. cit.," pp. 148, 153.

to the Church in these matters and to remove the Church from the political influence of the government of Philip II.[31]

The Nuncio, Castagna, informed Philip II of the intention of the Pope on October 11 and again on November 20, 1568. Philip II refused to accept the Pope's plan. Unfortunately, Cardinal Spinoza, President of the Spanish Council of the Indies also rejected the policy of direct control of ecclesiastical affairs as demanded by Pius V.[32]

In January of 1569, Cardinal Amulio was still waiting for a final answer from the King and his Council. But the King did not change his attitude toward the Holy See. Cardinal Spinoza played a very influential role informing the King's adverse attitude. The commission finally ceased to function at the beginning of 1569. It was not revived in any stable manner, not even after the death of Cardinal Spinoza in 1572, and not even under Sixtus V (1585-1590).[33]

ARTICLE 3. COMMISSION UNDER GREGORY XIII

The commission of Pius V did not survive under Gregory XIII. *"Se infatti sotto il pontificato di Gregorio XIII non fu ristabilita la Congregazione fondata da San Pio V, 'per la conversione degli infedeli in generale.'"* [34] Gregory XIII, however, established a new commission for a similar purpose. It consisted of three Cardinals (De Medici, Carafa, and Santorio, known as Cardinal Santa Severina) on June 10, 1573. The suggestion to form this commission was made to the Pope by Cardinal Santorio.[35] Wernz-Vidal,[36] Monin,[37] and V. Martin[38] cite the erection of

[31] *Ibid.,* p. 153.

[32] *Ibid.,* p. 157.

[33] Castelucci, "art. cit.," pp. 159-161.

[34] Castelucci, *Il resveglio,* p. 164.

[35] Vromant, *Ius Missionariorum de Personis* (Louvain: Museum Lessianum, 1935), p. 6 (hereafter referred to as *De Personis*).

[36] *Ius Canonicum* (7 vols. in 8, Romae: Apud Aedes Universitatis Gregorianae, 1923-1943), Vol. II, 3. ed., n. 495; cf. also Wernz, *Ius Decretalium* (6 vols., Romae et Prati, 1898-1905), II, 764.

[37] *De Curia Romana,* p. 66.

[38] *Les Congrégations Romaines* (Paris, 1930), p. 137.

this commission by Gregory XIII and mention its twofold purpose: (1) to assist in the preservation of the faith among Catholics of the Greek rite; and (2) to reunite schismatics and heretics with the Catholic Church. Monin's opinion [39] appears to be that the commission was engaged in several matters pertaining to the general propagation of the faith, but V. Martin [40] definitely asserts that it was a *Congregatio de rebus Graecorum*. Bertini [41] says of the commission that Gregory XIII erected the Congregation for the Greeks only, *soltanto* (explaining that it was established *pro reformatione Graecorum in Italia existentium et monacorum S. Basilii*).

Wernz-Vidal,[42] Monin,[43] and V. Martin [44] do not treat in detail the existence of this commission during the reign of Gregory XIII. They neither name cardinals nor state the year of its foundation. Monin [45] simply says that Clement VIII (1592-1605) confirmed the commission, increased the number of cardinals, and set it to active work.

V. Martin [46] gives the same account: *"Grégoire XIII érigea une congrégatione de rebus Graecorum, dont Clément VIII accrut l'autorité et accéléra les travaux. Elle cessa de fonctionner en 1605."* Wernz-Vidal [47] report the establishment of the commission by Gregory XIII.

These authors do not say anything about the existence of the

[39] *Op. cit.*, p. 66; cf. Vromant, *De Personis*, p. 6.

[40] *Les Congrégations Romaines*, pp. 137, 191; Castelucci, *Il risveglio*, pp. 164-165; Bertini, "art. cit.," p. 330; Schmidlin, *Catholic Mission History*, p. 257.

[41] "S.C. di Propaganda Fide," *Enciclopedia Cattolica*, IV, 330.

[42] *Ius Canonicum*, Vol. II, n. 495. Cf. Wernz, *Ius Decretalium*, II, 764.

[43] *De Curia Romana*, p. 66.

[44] *Les Congrégations Romaines*, pp. 136, 191.

[45] *Op. cit.*, p. 66.

[46] *Op. cit.*, pp. 136, 191.

[47] *Loc. cit.*: "Commissio trium Cardinalium a Gregorio XIII eo fine constituta, ut catholicos ritus graeci in fine conservaret et schismaticos ad Ecclesiam reduceret, est primum vestigium S.C. de Prop. Fide. Quae commissio a Clemente VIII compluribus cardinalibus aucta in perfectionem formam redacta est." Cf. Wernz, *Ius Decretalium*, II, 764.

commission during the pontificates of the four successors of Gregory XIII—Sixtus V (1585-1590), Urban VII (September 15, 1590–September 27, 1590), Gregory XIV (1590-1591), Innocent IX (October 29, 1591–December 30, 1591). Petrani affirms that Gregory XIII, under the inspiration of Santa Severina (Giulio Santorio), instituted the *Congregatio Graeca* (or simply *de rebus Graecorum*) in the year 1573, that the death of Gregory XIII hindered the progress of its work, and that it afterwards became extinct.[48]

Pastor, in giving information concerning the *Congregatio Graeca* erected by Gregory XIII, first mentions Cardinals Sirleto (1514-1585), Santorio († 1602), and Savelli († 1587) as the Pope's advisers in this matter. He then states:

> In 1573 he [Gregory XIII] formed these into a special Congregation to deal with the affairs of the Greeks. By their advice the Roman Catechism was translated into modern Greek, and in 1576 no less than 12,000 copies were sent to the Levant, together with a like number of copies of the decrees of the Council of Trent.[49]

As to the number of cardinals of that Congregation, Santorio's Consistorial diary under the date of June 10, 1573,[50] shows the appointment of four Cardinals (Savelli, Sirleto, Santorio and A. Carafa) to the *Congregatio Graecorum*. Pastor explains (1) that according to Santorio's *Autobiografia* five Cardinals belonged to the Congregation (Savelli, Sirleto, A. Carafa, Filippo Boncompagni, and Santorio) ; and (2) that Coquelines [51] gives other names in the *Annali di Gregorio XIII*.[52] The autobiography of Santorio shows still another member, one who is not a Cardinal—

---

[48] Petrani, "De Sacra Congregatione pro Ecclesia Orientali eiusque facultatibus," *Apollinaris*, X (1937), 28.

[49] Pastor, *The History of the Popes*, XX, 486.

[50] Tacchi Venturi, "Diario Consistoriale di Giulio Antonio Santori di Santa Severina," *Studie Documenti di Stora e Diritto* (Roma, 1880-   ), XXIV (1903), 135.

[51] Moroni, *Dizionario di Erudizione Storico-Ecclesiastica* (103 vols., Venezia: Della Tipografia Emiliana, 1840-1961), XVI, 241 (hereafter referred to as *Dizionario*).

[52] Cf. Pastor, *op. cit.*, XIX, 60.

the Archbishop of Corfù.[53] Some others, like Moroni[54] and Schmidlin,[55] mention the increase of the number of cardinals of the Congregation.

From the above facts, it is evident that the commission *Congregatio Graeca*, formed by Gregory XIII, is not the revivification of the commission of Pius V.

ARTICLE 4. RESTORATION OF THE COMMISSION OF PIUS V BY CLEMENT VIII

During the short tenure of the four Popes from 1585 to 1592 no mention of the commission of Gregory XIII can be found. However, the direction in apostolic affairs and in missionary organization was quite different under Clement VIII.[56]

On February 10, 1593, the first of several meetings took place. They were called *Congregationes super reformatione graecorum.*[57] These congregations are not to be taken in the sense of the Roman Congregations, but they were more or less synodal in character. A canonical congregation must have cardinals as the principal members,[58] but only one Cardinal, Santorio, presided at these meetings of bishops: Ludovico di Torres, Archbishop of Monreal (1584-1609) in Sicily, Gaspare Vivano, Bishop of Anagni

---

[53] Antonius Caucus was Archbishop of Corfù from May 29, 1560 to Nov. 29, 1577. Cf. Eubel, *Hierarchia Catholica Medii Aevi sive Summorum Pontificum, S.R.E. Cardinalium, Ecclesiarum Antistitum Series* (4 vols., Vols. I [1913] and II [1914] in 2. ed., edited by Conradus Eubel; Vol. III [1910] edited by Gulielmus Van Gulick–Conradus Eubel; Vol. IV [1935] edited by Patritius Gauchat under the title of *Hierarchia Catholica Medii et Recensioris Aevi sive Summorum Pontificum, S.R.E. Cardinalium, Ecclesiarum Antistitum Series;* Monasterii: Sumptibus et Typis Librariae Regensburgianae), III (1910), 194 (hereafter cited as *Hierarchia*).

[54] *Dizionario*, XVI, 241-242.

[55] "Die Gründung der Propagandakongregation (1622)," *Zeitschrift für Missionswissenschaft*, XII (1922), 2.

[56] Goyau, "Les Initiatives Belges dans la Fondation de la Propagande," *La Revue Générale* (Bruxelles, 1865-   ), CXII (1924), 11, 19-20.

[57] Staffa, "De Sacrae Congregationis pro Ecclesia Orientali competentia," *Apollinaris*, XI (1938), 360.

[58] *Bull. Rom.*, VIII, 986-987; Pastor, *The History of the Popes*, XXI, 250.

(1579-1605) in Latium, Italy,[59] and Owen, Bishop of Cassano in Calabria, Italy.[60] They were joined at the fourth meeting by Carlo Conti, Bishop of Ancona (1585-1616) in the Marches, Italy.[61]

On August 31, 1595, Clement issued a special instruction, the *Instructio super aliquibus ritibus Graecorum,* in order to reform certain complexities of the Greek rites. He made great use of the results of *Congregationes super reformatione graecorum.*[62] Again the matter must not be understood in the sense of a Roman Congregation as such.

Clement VIII finally restored the original commission of Pius V, which had been inactive for many years. The re-established Congregation encompassed the whole vast area of the missions, namely, from Northern Europe to the extreme limits of Africa, and from the West Indies to far-off Korea. It also became responsible for all aspects of support for the missions. So far as internal organization and the governing of mission works are concerned, this Congregation re-established by Clement VIII does not differ from the one reconstituted later by Gregory XV (1621-1623).[63] On Tuesday evening, August 10, 1599,[64] the members of the Congregation were appointed: Cardinal Santa Severina (Santorio), the Cardinal of Florence, cardinals Federico Borromeo, Archbishop of Milan (1564-1631), Alessandro de Medici

[59] Haine, *De la Cour Romaine* (Louvain, 1895), p. 249.

[60] Staffa, *loc. cit.;* Haine, *loc cit.;* Korolevskij, "L'Istruzione di Clemente VIII 'Super Aliquibus Ritibus Graecorum' (1595) e le Congregazioni per la Reforma dei Greci (1593)," *Bessarione* (Roma, 1896-), XXIX, 345, footnote n. 3.

[61] Staffa, *loc. cit.*

[62] Pastor, *The History of the Popes,* XXIV, 263.

[63] Staffa, "art. cit.," XI (1938), 360; Castelucci, "art. cit.," pp. 188, 192-193, 195; Bertini, "art. cit.," p. 330; Schmidlin, *Catholic Mission History,* p. 258.

[64] Lemmens, *Acta S. Congregationis de Propaganda Fide pro Terra Sancta Biblioteca Bio-Bibliografica della Terra Santa e dell' Oriente Francescano* (14 vols., edited by Girolamo Golubovich, Quaracchi presso Firenze, 1921-1936), I, 1, footnote n. 2 (hereafter referred to as *Acta*).

(1535-1605), Cesare Baronio (1538-1607), Alfonso Visconti (1552-1608), Silvio Antoniano (1540-1603), Roberto Bellarmino (1542-1621), Pietro Aldobrandini (1571-1621), and Cinzio Passeri-Aldobrandini (1551-1610), known as the Cardinal of St. George.[65]

The first meeting (as may be established from the original and authentic documents in the Archives of the Congregation for the Propagation of the Faith) was announced on that Tuesday evening in the presence of the pope. The Congregation would assemble before the pope on the next day, August 11, 1599 at 12:30 P.M. The second meeting took place on August 16; thereafter the meetings were held regularly in the house of Santorio at Monte Cavello, according to the wishes of the pope.[66]

Vromant,[67] Moroni,[68] and Benigni [69] mention that every week the commission met at the house of Santorio, and every fifteen days the members consulted with the pope. Pastor [70] asserts that it was planned to hold meetings twice a month, and that after each meeting Santorio reported to the pope, and then at the next assembly communicated the result of his audience to the Congregation. According to Castelucci, the meetings were held every two weeks during the summer months, and every week during the winter months. Once a month during the summer, and every fifteen days in the winter, the cardinals met in presence of the pope to elucidate important matters and to submit serious problems for solution. The conference generally took place on Monday, but if the cardinals were prevented from attending, it was postponed to the next day. These weekly meetings were held in

[65] Castelucci, *Il risveglio*, pp. 192-193. Cf. Dziob, *The Sacred Congregation for the Oriental Church*, The Catholic University of America Canon Law Studies, n. 214 (Washington, D. C.: The Catholic University of America Press, 1945), pp. 18-19 and footnotes nn. 101-104.

[66] Lemmens, *Acta*, I, 1, footnote n. 2; Moroni, *Dizionario*, XVI, 242; Pastor, *op. cit.*, XXIV, 266.

[67] *De Personis*, p. 7.

[68] *Dizionario*, XVI, 242.

[69] Benigni, "Sacred Congregation of Propaganda," *The Catholic Encyclopedia* (16 vols. and supplement I, II, New York, 1911), XII, 456.

[70] *Op. cit.*, p. 267.

the house of Santorio (the Cardinal of Santa Severina had given up his home at Piazza Navona and had acquired for his own use the Palazzo of Cardinal Cesi, at Monte Cavello). The monthly meetings used to be held in the Vatican. Unfortunately, this Congregation had a very short life. The last meeting held in the presence of the pope, *in palatio apostolico Vaticano apud S. Petrum in habitatione nova,* was on July 3, 1600.[71] Evidently the meetings did not work out according to the original schedule, for the *Acta,*[72] which are available up to August 14, 1600,[73] show only twelve meetings during the whole year.[74]

Bertini [75] asserts that the last meeting of the group was held on July 3, 1600. The last mention of the Congregation he refers to is in a document of March 29, 1601. Castelucci [76] holds that the Congregation was still mentioned in the Audiences of Santorio as late as March 29, 1601, but that after that date no official documents are available. Furthermore, Castelucci [77] adds that the Congregation had most certainly ceased to exist by the end of 1601. Nevertheless, according to the statement of Pastor,[78] the Congregation was still functioning in 1604. He proves

[71] Castelucci, "art. cit.," pp. 193, 195.

[72] Lemmens, *Acta,* I, 1; Schmidlin, "Eine Vorläuferin der Propaganda unter Klemens VIII," *Zeitschrift für Missionswissenschaft* (1921), XI, 233.

[73] Lemmens, *loc. cit.;* Schmidlin, "art. cit.," p. 233, footnote n. 7; Pastor, *op. cit.,* XXIV, 266-267.

[74] Schmidlin, *loc. cit.* Schmidlin omits August 11, for he began to list the meetings from the one at Santorio's house. In 1599, August 16, 30, September 20, November 24, December 13; in 1600, January 17, 31, February 28, July 3, 17, August 14. This demonstrates contrary to the assertion of Pastor (*op. cit.,* XXIV, 266): "Unfortunately only the notes of the first 10 meetings have been preserved").

[75] "Art. cit.," p. 330.

[76] *Il risveglio,* p. 197.

[77] *Loc. cit.*

[78] Pastor (*op. cit.,* XXIV, p. 575, n. 23) gives an extract of this letter of Francesco Maria Vialardo to the Duke of Mantua: ". . . Il card¹ᵉ di Perone sarà qui questa sera. Gioiosa è ammalato di lieve puntura, il Papa fa sborsare 50ᵐ duc¹¹ per il negotio dell' acqua di Ferrara, voule che si rimetta la congregatione de propaganda fide . . . ."

this by means of the letter of Francis Maria Vialardo sent to the Duke of Mantua (December 11, 1604).

V. Martin,[79] Moroni,[80] Monin,[81] and Petrani[82] state that the Congregation did not meet after the death of Clement VIII on March 3, 1605, while Benigni[83] asserts: "The death of Clement VIII revealed an essential weakness of the institution. It was a personal commission, depending for its very existence on the energy of its few members. Eventually the meetings of the three cardinals ceased; at the same time, an active propagation of the Catholic faith was kept up among both Protestants and non-Christians." It is not clear what Benigni means by "three cardinals," whether the three original cardinals at the time of the erection of the Congregation or the three surviving at the death of Clement VIII (1605).[84] It is certain, however, that there were nine cardinal members of the Congregation established by Clement VIII.[85] Of these, Cesare Baronio,[86] Alfonso Visconti,[87] Cinzio Passeri-Aldobrandini,[88] Pietro Aldobrandini,[89] Roberto Bellarmino,[90] and Federico Borromeo[91] outlived the pope.

No record is found in Lemmens' *Acta* after August 14, 1600,[92] although the Congregation evidently continued to exist. The death of Cardinal Santorio in 1602 caused an interruption in its activities. Pastor states: "As the presidency, and therefore the

[79] *Les Congrégations Romains*, pp. 137, 191.

[80] *Dizionario*, XVI, 242.

[81] *De Curia Romana*, p. 66.

[82] "Art. cit.," p. 29.

[83] "Art. cit.," XII, 456.

[84] Dziob, *op. cit.*, pp. 21-22.

[85] Cf. *supra*, pp. 12-13.

[86] Died on June 30, 1607: *Hierarchia*, IV, 5, n. 13.

[87] Died on September 19, 1608: *ibid.*, p. 6, n. 24.

[88] Died on January 1, 1610: *ibid.*, p. 4, n. 4.

[89] Died on February 10, 1621: *ibid.*, p. 4, n. 3.

[90] Died on September 17, 1621: *ibid.*, p. 6, n. 30.

[91] Died on September 21, 1631: *Hierarchia*, III, 58, n. 26.

[92] Lemmens, *Acta*, I, 1.

Acta now passed into the hands of another Cardinal, this explains their disappearance." [93]

Although the activity of the Congregation may have fallen into abeyance, nevertheless, from a document which Pastor quotes,[94] it is evident that a Congregation named *"de Fide Propaganda"* existed under Paul V (1605-1621). The document further relates that in this Congregation discussions were held and resolutions adopted concerning the plan to be followed in those places where some one was trying to teach and spread the faith. Moreover, some of the members of Clement VIII's Congregation are in the list of cardinals of this Congregation: the Cardinal of Ascoli, the Cardinal of St. Cecilia, Aldobrandini (Pietro Aldobrandini), San Giorgio (Cinzio Aldobrandini), Paravicino,[95] Arigonio,[96] Visconti (Alfonso),[97] Spinelli,[98] Monopoli,[99] Seraphino,[100] and San Cesario.[101]

Thus, the Congregation did exist, even though its central directorate may not have been very active. This Congregation foreshadowed the Congregation for the Propagation of the Faith (1622) in name, in purpose, and in procedure.[102]

[93] *The History of the Popes,* XXIV, 268, footnote n. 1. Pastor adds: "But perhaps it will still be possible to find them."

[94] *Op. cit.,* XXVII, 130, footnote n. 2. "La Congregazione detta de Fide Propaganda. Qui si discorre e risolve del modo che si de' tenere in quei luoghi ove si sente che la fede cattolica habbia qualche principio e che vi sia chi cerchi istruirla e propaganda."

[95] Octavianus Paravicinus died in 1611. Cf. Van Gulick-Eubel, *Hierarchia,* III, 60, n. 2.

[96] Pompeius Arrigonius (Arrigoni, Arigonus) died on April 4, 1616. Cf. Gauchat, *Hierarchia,* IV, 5, n. 19.

[97] Died on September 19, 1608. *Ibid.,* p. 6, n. 24.

[98] Philippus Spinellus died on May 25, 1616. *Ibid.,* p. 7, n. 39.

[99] Anselmus Marzatus Monopolitanus died on August 17, 1607. *Ibid.,* p. 8, n. 51.

[100] Seraphinus Olivarius died on February 10, 1609. *Ibid.,* p. 7, n. 36.

[101] Silvester Aldobrandinus, called the Cardinal of St. Cesario from his title S. Caesarei in Palatio. Died on January 28, 1612. *Ibid.,* p. 6, n. 35. Cf. Dziob, *op. cit.,* pp. 22-23 and footnotes nn. 131-137 for this section.

[102] Pastor, *op. cit.,* XXIV, 267; Schmidlin, "art. cit.," XI, 233.

CHAPTER II

ESTABLISHMENT AND COMPETENCE OF THE CONGREGATION BEFORE THE CODE OF CANON LAW

ARTICLE 1. ESTABLISHMENT OF THE CONGREGATION BY GREGORY XV

On January 6, 1622,[1] Gregory XV established the Congregation for the Propagation of the Faith as a special body with the explicit object of advancing and supervising the missions. This was to be a revival of the Commission begun under Clement VIII in 1599.[2] It consisted of thirteen cardinals, two prelates, and a Secretary General.[3] The first general assembly of the Congregation was held on January 14, 1622, at the palace of Cardinal de Saulis.[4]

The newly appointed members of the Congregation decreed that a letter should be written to all the Apostolic Nuncios inquiring about the status of religion in their territories. Moreover, the Apostolic Nuncios were asked to inform the Congregation of the methods by which the Catholic faith might be promoted in their territories. At the same meeting, the Congregation decided that a bull for the establishment of the Congregation, including its faculties and privileges, should be formulated just as had been done by the pope in erecting other Congregations.[5]

---

[1] Schmidlin, "Die Gründung der Propagandakongregation (1622)," *Zeitschrift für Missionswissenschaft*, XII (1922), 5; Pastor, *op. cit.*, XXVII, 132; S.C.P.F., acta, 1622—*Coll. S.C.P.F.*, I, n. 1.

[2] Pastor, *op. cit.*, p. 131; Castelucci, "art. cit.," p. 195.

[3] S.C.P.F., 1622—*Coll. S.C.P.F.*, I, n. 1; Schmidlin, *loc. cit.*; Pastor, *loc. cit.*

[4] *Coll. S.C.P.F.*, I, n. 1; Moroni, *Dizionario*, XVI, 243.

[5] S.C.P.F., 15 ian. 1622—*Coll. S.C.P.F.*, I, n. 2.

On June 22, 1622, Gregory XV officially established the Congregation for the Propagation of the Faith by the constitution *Inscrutabili*. In it he published the names of the members and announced in detail the work of the Congregation in the promotion of mission activities throughout the whole world.[6]

> Cardinales autem, quos sancta huic negotio praefecimus, sunt qui sequuntur: Antonius Ostiensis Saulius,[7] Odoardus Sabinensis Farnesius,[8] Octavius Praenestinus,[9] Episcopi; Bandinus Franciscus S. Praxedis de Surdis,[10] Maphaeus S. Honuphrii Barberinus,[11] Ioannes Garzias SS. Quatuor Coronatorum Millinus,[12] Gaspar Sanctae Crucis in Hierusalem Borgia,[13] Robertus S. Alexii Ubaldinus,[14] Scipio S. Susannae,[15] Petrus S. Salvatoris in Lauro Valerius,[16] Itelius Fridericus S. Laurentii in Pane et Perna de Zolleren,[17] Ludovicus S. Mariae transpontinae Ludovisius,[18] et Franciscus S. Matthaei,[19] Titulorum Presbyteri Cardinales, Sacratus, Nuncupati. Praelati vero, dilecti filii Io. Baptista Vives [20] in utraque Signatura nostra Referendarius, et Io. Baptista

[6] *Bullarium Pontificium Sacrae Congregationis de Propaganda Fide* (5 vols. and appendices, Romae, 1839-1841), I, 26-30 (hereafter referred to as *Bull. S.C.P.F.*); Gregory XV, const. *Inscrutabili*, 22 iun. 1622—*Coll. S.C.P.F.*, I, n. 3.

[7] The above quotation is taken from *Coll. S.C.P.F.*, I, n. 3. Informations for each the above named may be found in the sources and reference work cited next to each number. *Fontes*, n. 200, § 10; *Bull. S.C.P.F.*, I, n. 29. Cf. *Hierarchia*, III, 57, n. 20.

[8] *Fontes, loc. cit.; Bull. S.C.P.F., loc. cit.* Cf. *Hierarchia*, III, 60, n. 4.

[9] *Hierarchia*, IV, 4, n. 8.

[10] *Ibid.*, p. 6, n. 32.

[11] *Ibid.*, p. 10, n. 4.

[12] *Ibid.*, p. 10, n. 5.

[13] *Ibid.*, p. 12, n. 29.

[14] *Ibid.*, p. 12, n. 33.

[15] *Ibid.*, p. 13, n. 47.

[16] *Ibid.*, p. 14, n. 53.

[17] *Ibid.*, p. 14, n. 54.

[18] *Ibid.*, pp. 15-16, n. 1.

[19] *Ibid.*, p. 16, n. 3.

[20] *Fontes*, n. 200, § 11; *Bull. S.C.P.F.*, I, 29.

Anqucchius [21] Secretarius noster, ac Sedis Apostolicae Notarius, et Dominicus a Iesu Maria [22] Ordinis Carmelitarum Discalceatorum Professor, et Vicarius Generalis.

The members held a meeting in the presence of the pope once a month, and twice a month *in domo antiquioris eorum* in order to discuss *omnia et singula negotia* concerning the propagation of the faith in the whole world.[23]

ARTICLE 2. COMPETENCE OF THE CONGREGATION IN THE CONSTITUTION *Inscrutabili*

The Congregation for the Propagation of the Faith exercised extensive jurisdiction in the areas designated as missionary territory. According to the constitution *Inscrutabili* of Gregory XV, the Congregation had the full, free and sufficient authority, faculty, and power to perform, manage, treat, do, and execute all matters whatsoever pertaining to the propagation of the faith throughout the world.[24]

The faculty, authority, and power of this Congregation was guaranteed by the abrogation of all existing legislation to the contrary. The constitution took effect, notwithstanding privileges, indults, and apostolic letters conceded to any orders, congregations, societies and institutes, so that by law anything that conflicted with its provisions had to give way.[25]

[21] *Fontes, loc. cit.; Bull. S.C.P.F., loc. cit.*

[22] It is not listed in the list of Pastor (*The History of the Popes*), XXVII, 132, but found in Moroni, *Dizionario,* XVI, 243. It should be noted here that the Thomas a Jesu is not in the list of the members.

[23] *Coll. S.C.P.F.,* I, n. 3—*Bull. S.C.P.F.,* I, 28—*Fontes,* n. 200, § 8. The senior member was Cardinal de Saulis, who was the first Prefect of the Congregation.

[24] *Coll. S.C.P.F.,* I, n. 3—*Bull. S.C.P.F.,* I, 28—*Fontes,* n. 200, § 28: "Non enim eis, tam praemissa, quam omnia et singula alia desuper necessaria et opportuna etiam si talia fuerint quae specialem, specificam, et expressam requirant mentionem, faciendi, gerendi, tractandi, agendi et exsequendi plenam, liberam, et amplam facultatem, auctoritatem, et potestatem, apostolica auctoritate, earumdem tenore praesentium concedimus et impartimus."

[25] *Coll. S.C.P.F.,* I, n. 3—*Bull. S.C.P.F.,* I, 29: "Non obstantibus quibusvis Constitutionibus et ordinationibus Apostolicis, privilegiis quoque, indultis, et literis Apostolicis, quibusvis Ordinibus, Congregationibus, Societati-

As to the extent of the competence of the Congregation, Cappello,[26] De Meester,[27] Meehan,[28] and Bouix [29] attribute to the Congregation an exclusive competence in all affairs and a most ample power in all ecclesiastical causes affecting the territories of the missions.

M. Martin,[30] a pre-Code author, writes: "Hence what the various Congregations were accustomed to do for those countries subject to the common law of the Church, the same the Propaganda Congregation has done for those countries placed under its jurisdiction. It has been therefore a common saying regarding the Propaganda, that *'ceteras Congregationes habet in ventre.'*" Then, he adds, more specifically, that the general practice for the solution of doctrinal questions was to refer them to the Holy Office. However, the Congregation was not under obligation to do this, since no prohibition was issued to prevent the giving of doctrinal solution.

Sipos,[31] a post-Code author, similarly asserts that the Congregation had jurisdiction for the solution of doctrinal matters up to the curial reorganization under Pius X.

Wernz [32] affirms that all ecclesiastical matters in mission territories were subject to the Congregation for the Propagation of the Faith, except for cases pertaining to the Sacred Penitentiary.

---

bus et Institutis, sub quibuscumque tenoribus et formis, ac cum quibusvis, etiam derogatoriarum derogatoriis, aliisque efficacioribus, et insolitis clausulis ac irritantibus, et aliis decretis, in genere vel in specie, ac alias in contrarium praemissorum quomodolibet concessis, confirmatis, et innovatis. Quibus omnibus et singulis, eorum omnium tenores praesentibus pro plene et sufficienter expressis, et ad verbum insertis habentes, illis alias in suo robore permansuris hac vice dumtaxat specialiter, et expresse derogamus caeterisque contrariis quibuscumque."

26 *Op. cit.,* I, 232.

27 *Iuris Canonici et Iuris Canonico-civilis Compendium* (3 vols. in 4, Burgis, 1923), II, 84.

28 *Compendium Iuris Canonici* (Roffae, 1899), p. 66.

29 *Tractatus de Curia Romana* (Paris, 1859), p. 232.

30 *The Roman Curia* (New York, 1913), pp. 70-71.

31 *Enchiridion Iuris Canonici* (Pécs: Typographia Haladás, 1936), p. 212.

32 *Ius Decretalium,* II, 765.

The same opinion is held by Forget [33] and Ojetti. [34]   Monin [35] and V. Martin [36] declare that the questions of the internal forum were excluded from the competence of the Congregation.   They add, moreover, that the Congregation for the Propagation of the Faith was accustomed to remit doubts and problems for solution (matters of dogma, rites, and sacraments) to the respective Congregations, though there was no obligation for the Congregation to do this.

Bargilliat, [37] Lega, [38] and Santi-Leitner [39] state that the Congregation had most ample powers for all ecclesiastical affairs, of whatever species, in mission regions.   They, then, explain that the Congregation was accustomed (*solet*) to remit doctrinal matters to the Holy Office and that the Congregation requested (*exposcit*) the solution of questions concerning the forum of conscience from the Sacred Penitentiary.

According to these authors, there was no obligation for the Congregation to remit matters to the Holy Office.   The use of *solet,* moreover, indicates that this was not necessarily always done.   It is not clear whether there was an obligation to recur to the Sacred Penitentiary, or whether it was the general practice of the Congregation to do so without obligation just as in the case of the Holy Office.

Sebastianelli [40] make no distinction between *solet* and *exposcit.*

[33] "Congrégations Romaines," *Dictionnaire de Théologie Catholique* (14 vols. in 26, Paris: Letouzey et Ane, 1903-1939), III (1931), 1113.

[34] *De Romana Curia* (Romae, 1910), n. 76.

[35] *De Curia Romana,* p. 68.

[36] *Les Congrégations Romaines,* p. 142.

[37] *Praelectiones Iuris Canonici* (2 vols., Paris, 1905), Vol. I, n. 465, 2°: "Quod si agatur de negotio quod materiam fidei directe respicit, S. Congregatio illud ad S. Officium remittere solet.   Si vero negotium conscientiae forum directe attingat, a S. Poenitentiaria opportunum remedium vel solutionem quaestionis exposcit."

[38] *Praelectiones in Textum Iuris Canonici de Iudiciis Ecclesiasticis* (4 vols., Romae, 1898), II, 140-141.

[39] *Praelectiones Iuris Canonici* (3 vols., Romae, 1904-1905), I, 313.

[40] *Praelectiones Iuris Canonici* (3 vols., Romae, 1905), I, 87: "At solet haec Congregatio remittere ad S. Officium negotia directe ad fidem spec-

He simply uses *solet,* thus holding that the Congregation was accustomed to recur to the respective Congregation concerned with the affairs in question.

Laurentius,[41] on the contrary, tries to limit the jurisdiction of the Congregation for the Propagation of the Faith to the external forum, while Craisson affirms a competence in both the internal and external fora.   The latter says that doctrinal questions and cases of conscience presented by missionaries were solved by the Congregation for the Propagation of the Faith.[42]

What conclusion may be offered?   According to the constitution *Inscrutabili,* Gregory XV required that only *graviora* matters be remitted to him.   He clearly did not limit any jurisdiction of the Congregation for the Propagation of the Faith on any species of mission affairs.   Hence, all ecclesiastical causes, no matter what their species be, which arose from the designated missionary regions were subject to the Congregation.   In all cases, the affairs from these territories were to be addressed to this Congregation.[43]

It should be noted here, however, that this Congregation was certainly accustomed to refer some specific matters to the respective Congregation concerned.[44]   In such cases, the reply was

tantia, ad S. Poenitentiariam casus et petitiones pro foro interno, ad S. Cong. Concilii, aut aliam competentem, solutionem dubiorum, quae ius commune attingunt."

[41] *Institutiones Iuris Ecclesiastici* (Friburgi Brisgoviae, 1903), n. 155.

[42] Craisson, *Manuale Iuris Canonici* (5. ed., 3 vols., Pictavii, 1877), Vol. I, n. 780.

[43] Smith, *Elements of Ecclesiastical Law* (3 vols., New York, 1887), Vol. I, n. 508: ". . . ecclesiastical matters from missionary countries must be referred exclusively to, and are arranged solely by the Propaganda.   Hence, of this Congregation it is said: Caeteras Congregationes habet in ventre, i.e., for missionary countries the Propaganda is the sole Congregation, combines in itself the powers and discharges the duties of functions not merely of several, but of all the other Congregations; so that while the priests and bishops of countries where canon law obtains must refer matters to the respective congregations, the priests and bishops of missionary countries must, in all cases, address themselves to the Propaganda, but to no other congregation."

[44] Simier, *La Curie Romaine* (Paris, 1908), pp. 46–47; V. Martin, *op. cit.,* p. 143; Monin, *De Curia Romana,* p. 68; Lega, *Praelectiones in Textum*

given to the Congregation for the Propagation of the Faith,
and the latter in turn forwarded it to the party concerned.[45]
Such procedures were usual or customary, but no obligation existed on the part of the Congregation. In fact this Congregation itself did also treat matters of faith, as is readily apparent
from its acts.[46] Moreover, that the Congregation for the Propagation of the Faith enjoyed such powers over matters of faith
is definitely established by the explicit curtailment of this right
by the constitution *Sapienti consilio,* issued on June 29, 1908.[47]

In favor of the jurisdiction of the Sacred Penitentiary over subjects of the Congregation for the Propagation of the Faith from
the time of the constitutions *Romanus Pontifex* (Innocent XII,
September 3, 1692) and *Pastor bonus* (Benedict XIV, April 13,
1744), are the following: (1) The statement at the beginning of the
constitution *Pastor bonus* concerning the wish of the popes from
early times for an Office of the Sacred Penitentiary to which all
the faithful from all over the world might have recourse is clearly
expressed.[48] (2) Both the constitution *Romanus Pontifex* and
the constitution *Pastor bonus* conclude with the confirmation of
the powers of the Sacred Penitentiary, notwithstanding any other
constitutions and ordinances to the contrary.[49] At any rate it
is difficult to make a definite assertion on either side, whether
matters of the internal forum had to be deferred to the Sacred
Penitentiary, or whether this was merely the customary practice.

Iuris Canonici de Iudiciis Ecclesiasticis, II, 140-141; Sebastianelli, *op. cit.,*
I, 87.

[45] *Bull. Rom.,* XII, 766-768. Cf. Monin, *op. cit.,* p. 68.

[46] *Collectanea S. Congregationis de Propaganda Fide* (Romae, 1893), Vol.
I, Pars III, De Fide de Moribus.

[47] Pius X, const. *Sapienti consilio,* 29 iun. 1908—*AAS,* I (1909), 12, n. 6,
ad 4: "Nihilominus, ut unitati regiminis consulatur volumus ut Congregatio de Propaganda Fide ad peculiares alias Congregationes deferat quaecumque aut fidem attingunt, aut matrimonium aut sacrorum rituum disciplinam."

[48] *Magnum Bullarium Romanum, seu eiusdem Continuatio* (19 toms. in
18, Luxemburgi, 1727-1754), XVI, 184-189.

[49] *Magnum Bullarium Romanum, seu eiusdem Continuatio,* VII, 190-192;
Bull. Rom., XX, 450-461.

What was the nature of the power which the Congregation for the Propagation of the Faith enjoyed at this period? Again there are divergent opinions. With reference to the judicial power of the Congregation, De Luca writes: *"Adhuc tamen, ad instar praesertim Congregationis Regularium, ab aliquo tempore, aliqua forensia, vel contentiosa negotia peragere, ac decidere cum eodem Congregationum summario, et extraiudiciali stylo, consuevit. . . ."* [50] Criminal cases as well as contentious matters demanding a strict judicial process were thus treated by the Congregation for the Propagation of the Faith. This is verified in the study of the Roman Congregations in the *Analecta Iuris Pontificii* of 1857.[51] Monin also states that the Congregation had power to judge both contentious and criminal cases in mission areas.[52]

With reference to the legislative power of the Congregation for the Propagation of the Faith, the following may be noted. Antonio a S. Maria (Caballero), Prefect of the Chinese mission of the Franciscan Order, writing from the Philippine Islands in 1652, reported that some religious said that the resolutions and decrees of the Congregation for the Propagation of the Faith create only a probable opinion, as it were a simple declaration of the mind of the cardinals; consequently, the contrary opinion may also be defended. This report was read in the general assembly of the Congregation in the presence of the pope on July 30, 1652. Innocent X (1644-1655) thereupon confirmed the decree of Urban VIII, namely, that the decrees of the Congregation for the Propagation of the Faith, whenever they are approved by its Prefect, signed by its Secretary, and properly sealed, have the force of an apostolic constitution and must be observed inviolably by all persons.[53] This decree was again confirmed by

[50] De Luca, *Relatio Romanae Curiae Forensis*, discursus, XXIII, nn. 7, 8.

[51] "Des Congrégations Romaines et de Leur Pratique," *Analecta Iuris Pontificii* (Romae, 1855-1869, Paris, 1872-1891, and under the title *Analecta Ecclesiastica*, Paris, 1893-1911), II (1857), col. 2394, n. 113; col. 2413, n. 138.

[52] Monin, *op. cit.*, p. 68; Vromant, *De Personis*, p. 9.

[53] S.C.P.F., 30 iul. 1652—*Coll. S.C.P.F.*, I, n. 119; Lega, *op. cit.*, II, 143; Wernz-Vidal, *op. cit.*, p. 283.

the Congregation on May 15, 1779.[54] From this it may be concluded that the Congregation had true legislative power.[55]

Monin [56] raises the additional question whether the Congregation had such legislative power *iure proprio et ordinario*. Bouix [57] attributes proper and ordinary power to the Congregation in view of the terms of the constitution *Inscrutabili* of June 22, 1622, and Lega [58] rightly points out that the decree of Innocent X did not necessarily demand consultation with the Pope, but only the signs of authenticity (the signatures of the Prefect and Secretary and the seal). Hence, when it was evident through such signs that the *decreta* came from the Congregation for the Propagation of the Faith, they had the value of a constitution. If the general decrees were considered *graviora*, then of course pontifical approbation was required, in accordance with the constitution *Inscrutabili*.[59]

De iure, the Congregation for the Propagation of the Faith was established in 1622 as the exclusive organization for the government of the mission territories. *De facto*, however, this Congregation was not immediately able to exercise the full, free and ample authority, faculty, and the power to perform, manage, treat, do, and execute all matters pertaining to it in mission territories.

The first obstacle was the authority of the old religious orders (Franciscans, Dominicans, Carmelites, and Jesuits) which, even

[54] S.C.P.F., litt. 15 maii 1779—*Coll. S.C.P.F.* (1893), I, n. 11.

[55] Wernz-Vidal, *loc. cit.*; Baart, *The Roman Court*, p. 213; Bouix, *Tractatus de Curia Romana*, pp. 232-233; Hilling, *Procedure at the Roman Curia*, p. 83; Lega, *Praelectiones in Textum Iuris Canonici de Iudiciis Ecclesiasticis*, II, 142-143, 363-370; Laurentius, *op. cit.*, p. 124, n. 155; Monin, *De Curia Romana*, p. 68, footnote n. 1, stated: "Hinc concluserunt quidam hanc S.C. habere etiam potestatem legislativam." Similarly, Vromant, *De Personis*, p. 9, after mentioning the decree of July 30, 1652, concluded: ". . . quidem concluserunt hanc S.C. habere etiam potestatem legislativam pro universis terris missionum."

[56] *Op. cit.*, p. 68, footnote n. 1.

[57] *Op. cit.*, p. 233.

[58] *Op. cit.*, II, 366.

[59] *Coll. S.C.P.F.*, I, n. 3.

after the year 1622, still used the privileges and faculties granted by the popes prior to the Congregation's establishment. The religious superiors continued to nominate vicars apostolic, give faculties, direct, transfer, and correct their subjects.[60]

The right of Royal Patronage also afforded a hindrance to the Congregation for the Propagation of the Faith. Portugal excluded the Congregation from the exercise of authority in the areas from Mauretania to the Cape of Good Hope, and from the Persian Gulf to the Molucca Islands and Japan. Spain similarly excluded the Congregation from authority over all Latin America and the Philippine Islands.[61] The competence of the Congregation, moreover, was not exclusive of the rights of residential bishops nominated by Royal Patronage. These bishops educated their own subjects and ordained them, gave faculties, assigned offices, received missionaries, and assigned the latter without any communication with the Congregation. In view of the actual situation, there was a grave struggle over the efforts of the Congregation for the Propagation of the Faith to place a new hierarchy in mission lands.[62]

The right of Royal Patronage was a right of presentation to benefices, including the appointment of bishops, and embraced the exclusive power to send missionaries to the territories of the colonies.[63] The series of papal bulls granting these rights began with Nicholas V's *Dum diversas* of June 18, 1452 (for Portugal) [64] and Alexander VI's *Inter caetera* of May 4, 1493 (for Spain).[65]

[60] Masarei, *De Missionum Institutione ac de Relationibus inter Superiores Missionum et Superiores Religiosos* (Romae: Apud Institutum Graphicum Tibernium, 1940), pp. 62-63 (hereafter cited as *De Missionum Institutione*).

[61] Masarei, *De Missionum Institutione*, pp. 63-64.

[62] Masarei, *De Missionum Institutione*, p. 65; Latourette, *A History of Christian Missions in China* (New York: Macmillan, 1929), pp. 113-114, 124, 126, 240, 241.

[63] Grentrup, *Ius Missionariorum* (Steyl-Holland, 1925), pp. 196, 199, 232.

[64] *Bullarium Patronatus Portugaliae Regum*, Tomus I, p. 22; cf. Grentrup, *op. cit.*, p. 106.

[65] *Bull. Rom.*, V, 361.

To overcome the difficulties arising from the rights of Royal Patronage, the Congregation departed from the common law by substituting for the ordinary hierarchy vicars and prefects apostolic. The latter ruled their territories with delegated power (at that time) in the name of the pope. They were subject to the Congregation only and were independent of Patronage and also of privileges conceded to regulars.[66]

The definite beginning of this new hierarchical policy dates from the brief *Super cathedram* of Alexander VII, issued on September 9, 1659. Francis Pallu, of the newly founded Paris Foreign Mission Society, was appointed vicar apostolic of Tonking and the neighboring provinces of Cochin and Nanking, China. He was granted broad faculties and privileges: " . . . *non obstantibus concessionibus privilegiis etc. quibuscunque factis . . . ceterisque contrariis quibuscunque.*" [67]

The new hierarchical organization became permanent for the Far East, and the policy succeeded in bringing about the appointment of ecclesiastical superiors and the immediate administration of the missions under the control of the Congregation for the Propagation of the Faith.[68] On the other hand, many popes, from Innocent IV (1243-1254) to Clement VIII (1592-1605), had granted various faculties to regulars to facilitate the work of the missions.[69] These of course stood in the way of the complete exercise of the authority of the Congregation. The following three observations of Raymond Caron (1653) may give some idea of the wide faculties and privileges possessed by regulars.[70]

(1) The regular missionaries in places far removed from Rome had pontifical authority in both fora, insofar as they were concerned with the conversion of the native population.

---

[66] Masarei, *De Missionum Institutione,* pp. 72-73; Vromant, *Ius Missionariorum—Introductio et Normae Generales* (Louvain, 1934), p. 24.

[67] *Ius Pontificium de Propaganda Fide* (7 vols., Romae, 1888), Pars I, Vol. I, 313 (hereafter referred to as De Martinis, *Ius Pontificium*).

[68] S.C.P.F., 3 mart. 1766—*Coll. S.C.P.F.*, I, n. 463; II, n. 1314.

[69] Vromant, *op. cit.*, p. 21.

[70] Caron, *Apostolatus Evangelicus* (Antwerpiae, 1653), p. 135.

    (2) The regulars could do whatever they judged expedient for the expansion of the faith.

    (3) The regular missionaries were considered quasi-legates of the pope.[71]

In addition, regular superiors general, including the General of the Jesuits, had authority to establish missions and to give faculties necessary for the *cura animarum* to missionaries subject to them.[72]

When the Congregation for the Propagation of the Faith began to centralize all mission administration under its own authority, difficulties arose, since the regulars believed they were still in possession of their privileges. The Congregation, however, decreed that regular superiors were required to present their missionaries to the Congregation for examination and approval before being sent to the missions.[73] Moreover, decrees of July 20, 1628, and of January 30, 1629, insisted that regulars should not be recalled from the missions by their superiors without the consent of the Congregation.[74] Another decree of December 5, 1640, emphasized that the Congregation had the right to supervise all the missions in the whole world, including all orders, congregations, societies, or institutes of whatever kind.[75]

The privileges of regulars gradually fell into desuetude, through the constant *praxis* of the Congregation, which insisted on its exclusive right to supervise the missions. The various decrees of the Congregation during the remainder of the century constantly urged the missionaries, regulars included, to abide by the common law in the exercise of their ministry, and reminded them all of their dependence upon the *ordinarius loci* in regard to the *cura animarum*.

---

[71] Grentrup, *op. cit.*, pp. 22-23; Vromant, *op. cit.*, pp. 30-31.

[72] Vermeersch, "Commentaria de formulis facultatum quas S.C.P.F. concedere solet," *Periodica de Re Canonica et Morali*, XI (1922), 37; Masarei, *De Missionum Institutione*, p. 52.

[73] S.C.P.F., 24 iun. 1623—*Coll. S.C.P.F.*, I, n. 6.

[74] S.C.P.F., 20 iun. 1628—*Coll. S.C.P.F.*, I, n. 40; S.C.P.F., 30 ian. 1629—*Coll. S.C.P.F.*, I, n. 46.

[75] S.C.P.F., 5 dec. 1640—*Coll. S.C.P.F.*, I, n. 101.

These developments may be traced in the various decrees of the Congregation for the Propagation of the Faith:

June 24, 1623: Religious superiors must present their missionaries to the Congregation for examination and approval before sending them to the missions.[76]

July 20, 1626 and *January 30, 1629:* Regulars may not be recalled from the missions *inconsulta Propaganda.*[77]

September 13, 1669: In the constitution of Clement IX (1667-1669) *Speculatores,* the questions proposed by the vicars apostolic of Tonking, Cochin and Nanking, China, concerning the subordination of regulars to the vicar apostolic were answered. The pope stated that all religious of any order, congregation or institute, whether sent by their superiors, the Congregation, or the pope, were bound to present to the vicar apostolic testimonial letters attesting to their commission, destination, and deputation. Those who refused to do so could be prohibited from using the faculties conferred in their letters. Regulars also had to seek permission to use their faculties from the vicar apostolic. Furthermore, in regard to parochial matters, regulars were subject to visitation and correction by the vicar apostolic and they were not to build churches without permission. In case of conflicts, the vicar apostolic, as a delegate of the Holy See, had the right and duty to decide and settle the problem in question. Grave matters were to be referred to the Holy See.[78]

It appears from this that the faculties originally held by regulars were still used by them. Now they simply needed permission to make use of them. Yet in many cases they were in fact dependent on the vicars apostolic:

September 13, 1669: Regulars were not to use their faculties, unless they first obtained permission from the vicar.[79]

February 14, 1702: No missionaries, secular or regular, including the Jesuits, notwithstanding their privileges, were al-

---

[76] S.C.P.F., 24 iun. 1623—*Coll. S.C.P.F.,* I, n. 6.

[77] *Coll. S.C.P.F.,* I, nn. 40, 46.

[78] Clement IX, const. *Speculatores,* 13 sept. 1669—*Coll. S.C.P.F.,* I, n. 186—*Fontes,* n. 245, ad 2.

[79] *Loc. cit.*

lowed to administer the sacraments or perform parochial duties without the permission of the vicar apostolic in whose territory they were working.[80]

September 11, 1745: Benedict XIV (1740-1758) confirmed the decree of the Congregation for the Propagation of the Faith (August 16, 1745) concerning the dispute between the Franciscans and the vicar apostolic of England. Regulars, including Jesuits, had to obtain faculties from the vicar apostolic of the territory.[81] The same pope in his encyclical *Apostolicum ministerium* of May 30, 1753, for the missions of England, clearly asserted the revocation of the faculties of the regulars.[82]

Thus, the Congregation for the Propagation of the Faith gradually vindicated its exclusive authority. A final regulation may be mentioned. The norms given in the constitution of Leo XIII (1878-1903) *Romanos Pontifices*, on May 8, 1881, had to be observed in judging the privilege of exemption and what this exemption embraced for regulars in the missions.[83] When religious were sent to a mission entrusted to their order by the Holy See, the order was to present them to the vicar apostolic who approved them and gave them jurisdiction and the necessary faculties. Regulars were totally dependent on the vicar apostolic as regards the *cura animarum* and the administration of the sacraments and other cases mentioned in law.

Article 3. Congregations and Commissions Formerly Connected with the Congregation

In the course of its history, the Congregation for the Propagation of the Faith had several other bodies connected with it or related to its competence. To begin with, the *Congregatio particularis pro Sinis* appears for the first time in the *Collectanea S.C.P.F.* on January 13, 1665, and the last mention of this Congregation is in a document of the same collection dated January

---

[80] S.C.P.F., 14 febr. 1702—*Coll. S.C.P.F.*, I, n. 253.

[81] *Bull. S.C.P.F.*, IV, 303-318.

[82] Benedict XIV, ep. encycl. *Apostolorum ministerium*, 30 maii 1753—*Fontes*, n. 425, § 10; cf. Masarei, *De Missionum Institutione*, pp. 90-91.

[83] Leo XIII, const. *Romanos pontifices*, 8 maii 1881—*Coll. S.C.P.F.*, II, n. 1552—*Fontes*, n. 252; S.C.P.F., 1 sept. 1881—*Coll. S.C.P.F.*, II, n. 1558.

21, 1856. The special purpose of the Congregation was to supervise mission problems in China.[84]

In addition, three special Commissions were instituted: The *Commissio ad revisendas constitutiones Institutorum religiosorum a S.C.P.F. dependentium* was constituted to supervise religious houses in the territories of missions. After the constitution *Sapienti consilio* of June 29, 1908, the Congregation for the Propagation of the Faith had jurisdiction over religious only as missionaries. *"Haec erant instituta quae vel in territorio huic congregationi subjecto domum matricem vel generaliciam habebant; vel quae fine sibi proprio et peculiari ad missiones destinabantur."* [85] The other two Commissions were the *Commissio ad revisendas religiones dioecesium et vicariatuum Apostolicorum a S.C.P.F. dependentium super statu eorum ecclesiae,* and the *Commissio super revisione synodorum provincialium.*[86]

During the pontificate of Urban VIII (1623-1644), two Congregations for Oriental matters were instituted within the Congregation for the Propagation of the Faith. In 1627, the Pope named a number of cardinals of the latter to deal with more serious questions affecting Orientals.[87] This body was called the *Congregatio super dubiis orientalium.* In addition, Urban VIII established the *Congregatio super correctione Euchologii Graecorum,* to correct the liturgical books written in the Greek language.[88]

In order to further the progress of this work with the Greek

---

[84] S.C.P.F., 13 ian. 1665—*Coll. S.C.P.F.,* I, n. 159; S.C.P.F., 21 ian. 1856—*Coll. S.C.P.F.,* I, n. 1119.

[85] Vromant, *De Personis,* p. 13; Ojetti, *op. cit.,* n. 74: "Missionarii qua religiosi, inde ab edita constitutione piana *Sapienti Consilio,* pendent quoque sicut ceteri religiosi, a S.C. Religiosorum. Quaedam tamen exceptiones, ex particulari concessione S. Sedis, decursu temporum fuerunt iterum toleratae (cf. Decretum quo Congregatio Missionariorum B.M.V. de Scheut obnoxia fit iurisdictioni S.C.P.F.: *AAS* [1921], 354)."

[86] Vromant, *loc. cit.*

[87] Staffa, "De Sacrae Congregationis pro Ecclesia Orientali competentia," *Apollinaris,* XI (1938), 361; Monin, *De Curia Romana,* p. 270; Martin, *op. cit.,* p. 191.

[88] Pius IX, const. *Romani pontifices,* 6 ian. 1862—*Fontes,* n. 531.

liturgical books and with all the liturgical books of the Oriental
Church, a new Congregation distinct from the Congregation for
the Propagation of the Faith was later established by Clement
XI (1700-1721). It was called the *Congregatio super correctione
librorum orientalium* (1717), and had its own prefect and secretary. The new Congregation consisted of five cardinals as members, together with several theologians and other experts in Oriental rites and languages.[89] Furthermore, whenever individual
matters of importance concerning Orientals arose, the case was
invariably handed over to a particular commission within the
Congregation for the Propagation of the Faith.

On January 6, 1862, Pius IX (1846-1878) erected still another
new congregation in the constitution *Romani Pontifices*. Its name
was *Sacra Congregatio de Propaganda Fide pro negotiis ritus
orientalis*, and it constituted one section of the general Congregation for the Propagation of the Faith. At the same time, Pius
IX expressly decreed the suppression of the earlier *Congregatio
super correctione librorum orientalium*. The Prefect of the new
Congregatio pro negotiis ritus orientalis was the same as the
Prefect of the Congregation for the Propagation of the Faith itself. The organization consisted of several cardinals of the
latter, and it had its own secretary, consultors, and officials.[90]

On March 19, 1895, Leo XIII (1878-1903) instituted a pontifical commission by the *motu proprio Optatissime* to reconcile the
dissidents in schism or in heresy. This commission did not deal
exclusively with cases of Oriental schismatics and heretics. The
Pope designated a consultor in each case, and the one selected
was present *ex officio* at the meetings of the pontifical commission. Later, this commission was joined to the Congregation for
the Propagation of the Faith by the constitution *Sapienti consilio*.[91]

In the reform of the Roman Curia by Pius X (1903-1914), the
S.C. de Propaganda Fide pro negotiis ritus orientalis still re-

[89] *Loc. cit.*

[90] *Coll. S.C.P.F.*, I, n. 1223—*Fontes*, n. 531.

[91] Vromant, *op. cit.*, p. 13; *Leonis XIII Pontificis Maximi Acta* (23 vols.,
Romae, 1881-1905), XV, 80-82; *Acta Sanctae Sedis* (41 vols., Romae, 1865-
1908), XXVIII, 323 (hereafter referred to as *ASS*).

mained united with the Congregation for the Propagation of the Faith, but by the motu proprio *Dei providentis* of May 1, 1917, Benedict XV (1914-1922) established the *Sacra Congregatio pro Ecclesia Orientali.* The S.C.P.F. *pro negotiis ritus orientalis* ceased to exist on November 30, 1917, and on December 1, 1917, the new Congregation completely took over the work. It was entirely separate from and totally independent of the Congregation for the Propagation of the Faith and was a new Congregation of the Roman Curia.[92]

ARTICLE 4. COMPETENCE OF THE CONGREGATION
IN THE CONSTITUTION *Sapienti Consilio*

On June 29, 1908, Pius X issued the constitution *Sapienti consilio* [93] as well as the related *Normae communes,*[94] followed by the *Normae peculiares* [95] on September 29, 1908. In addition, on January 7, 1909, the Consistorial Congregation decided twelve questions concerning the competence of the Congregation for the Propagation of the Faith.[96]

Until this new organization of the Roman Curia was set up by Pius X, the mission countries were under the exclusive regime of the Congregation for the Propagation of the Faith in accordance with the constitution *Inscrutabili* of Gregory XV.[97]

The centralization of the entire mission system under a single supreme authority certainly had many advantages. Several of

[92] Benedict XV, motu propr. *Dei providentis,* 1 maii 1917—*AAS,* IX (1917), 529-531—*Fontes,* n. 710.

[93] Pius X, const. *Sapienti consilio,* 29 iun. 1908—*AAS,* I (1909), 7-19.

[94] *Ordo servandus in Sacris Congregationibus, Tribunalibus, Officiis Romanae Curiae,* Pars prima, *Normae communes* (hereafter cited as *Normae communes*)—*AAS,* I (1909), 36-58.

[95] *Ordo servandus in Sacris Congregationibus Tribunalibus, Officiis Romanae Curiae,* Pars altera, *Normae peculiares* (hereafter cited as *Normae peculiares*)—*AAS,* I (1909), 59-108.

[96] S.C. Consist., *Dubia de competentia,* 7 ian. 1909—*AAS,* I (1909), 148-152.

[97] Grentrup, "Die rechtlichen Beziehungen der Missionsländer zur römischen Kurie in der Gegenwart," *Archiv für katholisches Kirchenrecht,* XCIII (1913), 278.

these follow: (1) The single system achieved a substantial simplicity of communication in mission matters; (2) The special conditions of the mission territories were supervised in all directions by the supreme authority and they could be considered correctly in legislation, jurisdiction, and administration; (3) The material and spiritual promotion of the missions could be accomplished methodically and with uniformity.[98]

To these advantages, however, were opposed rather serious disadvantages especially in view of the condition of the time: (1) The Congregation for the Propagation of the Faith was overloaded.   If the words of the constitution *Sapienti consilio,*[99] *"aliae* [i.e., *congregationes] negotiis obruuntur,"* would apply to any of the Roman Congregations, it would especially be the case with the Congregation for the Propagation of the Faith; (2) The professional knowledge regarding individual matters could not be built up in the Congregation for the Propagation of the Faith to the same extent as was the case in other Congregations, to each of which was entrusted a uniform, clearly delimited field of action.   Therefore, the Congregation for the Propagation of the Faith was often led to request the assistance of other Congregations.   For instance, almost all questions regarding rites or indulgences were submitted to the Congregations appointed for those matters; (3) Because of the territorial division of the Church into the two parts, duplicate work had to be performed; (4) The desirable uniformity of the Church was not sufficiently guaranteed with regard to ecclesiastical jurisdiction and legislation.[100]   This is also mentioned in the constitution *Sapienti consilio,*[101] when it states, *"ut unitati regiminis consulatur . . . ;"* (5) The union of the mission territories with the other part of the Church was not satisfactory.[102]

[98] *Ibid.,* p. 279.

[99] Pius X, const. *Sapienti consilio,* 29 iun. 1908—*AAS,* I (1909), 8.

[100] Grentrup, "art. cit.," XCIII (1913), 279.

[101] Pius X, const. *Sapienti consilio,* I, 29 iun. 1908, n. 6, ad 4—*AAS,* I (1909), 12.

[102] Hilling, "Die rechtliche Stellung der Propagandakongregation nach der neuen Kurialreform Pius X," *Zeitschrift für Missionswissenschaft,* I (1911), 154.

These and similar reasons moved Pius X to restrict substantially the territory of the Congregation for the Propagation of the Faith and to change the position of the mission countries with regard to the Roman Curia as a whole, at least in the juridical aspect of this relationship.

The practical value of the reorganization of the Congregation for the Propagation of the Faith was seen in particular advantages: (1) Through the limitation of the territorial, personal, and material competence of the Congregation, the work of the Congregation for the Propagation of the Faith was substantially alleviated; (2) Because of the removal of a large complex of countries from the mission territories, the territory under the jurisdiction of the Congregation for the Propagation of the Faith became more uniform and harmonious. With the qualitative restriction of its affairs, the administrative apparatus of the Congregation could function more easily and securely.

These regulations completed the juridical reorganization of the Roman Curia.[103] According to the rules mentioned above, the Congregation for the Propagation of the Faith could no longer issue indults (such as the quinquennial faculties) to bishops not subject to its authority, as the Congregation had been doing. The Congregation henceforward could grant these faculties exclusively to its own subjects.[104] Another important restriction was introduced, namely, that the Congregation could not treat strictly judicial cases, but could settle only contentious cases by the administrative and disciplinary procedure.[105]

With regard to territories in which it was competent in the new disposition, the Congregation for the Propagation of the Faith included those parts of the world where the hierarchy had not yet been constituted or where the hierarchy was not well developed and the mission status still existed. This determination prevails today.

The mission territories now included, among others, Albania, the Antilles, Australia, Gibraltar, Greece, India, Iran, China,

---

[103] *Loc. cit.*

[104] *Normae peculiares,* cap. VII, art. VI, n. 3—*Fontes,* n. 6460.

[105] *Normae peculiares,* cap. II, n. 1; cap. III, art. II—*Fontes,* n. 6460—*AAS,* I (1909), 61, 64-65.

Japan, New Zealand, Palestine, and Turkey. On the other hand, Great Britain, Holland, Ireland, Scotland, Newfoundland, Luxemburg, Canada, and the United States, all mission territories in the nineteenth century, were so no longer. They were transferred from the control of the Congregation for the Propagation of the Faith to the other Congregations of the Roman Curia in the reorganization by Pius X.[106] Other provinces which were up to this time subject to the Congregation for the Propagation of the Faith, remained under its jurisdiction, as well as all vicariates and prefectures apostolic and all missions, even those which fell under the Congregation for Extraordinary Ecclesiastical Affairs.[107]

With regard to cases of doctrine, marriage, and sacred rites, the Congregation for the Propagation of the Faith was required by the *Sapienti consilio* to remit them to the proper Congregation.[108] According to the constitution, the *Congregatio de Propaganda Fide* may not, even within its own territories, transact business which relates to faith, marriage, or the discipline of sacred rites. Whenever such questions are proposed by anyone subject to the Congregation for the Propagation of the Faith, this Congregation must hand them over for solution to the proper Congregation.[109]

So far as those under its authority are concerned, the jurisdiction of the Congregation over religious missionaries was restricted to cases which pertained to the religious as missionaries. In cases which affected them as religious, the Congregation for Religious was alone competent.[110]

The special commission for the union of the dissident churches founded by Leo XIII was joined to the Congregation for the

---

[106] Pius X, const. *Sapienti consilio*, 29 iun. 1908—*AAS*, I (1909), 12, n. 6, ad 1, 2; *Sylloge Praecipuorum Documentorum Recentium Summorum Pontificum et S. Congregationis de Propaganda Fide* (Romae: Typis Polyglottis Vaticanis, 1939), n. 9 (hereafter referred to as *Sylloge*).

[107] *Ibid.*, n. 6, ad 3.

[108] *Ibid.*, n. 6, ad 4.

[109] *Loc. cit.*

[110] *Ibid.*, n. 6, ad 5.

Propagation of the Faith in 1908 and its affairs were attached to this Congregation.[111] The commission for the union of dissident churches had been erected by the *motu proprio Optatissime* of Leo XIII, March 19, 1895. The Roman Pontiff was its prefect, and it consisted of seven cardinals and several consultors.[112]

[111] *Ibid.,* n. 6, ad 6, 8.

[112] *ASS,* XXVIII (1895-1896), 323-324.

CHAPTER III

CONSTITUTION OF THE CONGREGATION

ARTICLE 1. INTERNAL ORGANIZATION AND FUNCTIONS

The Congregation was reorganized by the constitution *Sapienti consilio* of Pius X (June 29, 1908) and by the special rules for its general administration, in accordance with the *Ordo Servandus in S. Congregationibus* of September 29, 1908.[1] According to the arrangement contained in this document, as in the constitution *Inscrutabili* of Gregory XV (June 22, 1622), the deliberative powers, the supreme direction and handling of affairs, both spiritual and temporal, and the administration of estates and revenues, pertain to the *plenus Conventus* of the cardinals who compose the Congregation for the Propagation of the Faith.[2]

The Congregation for the Propagation of the Faith as such consists of the cardinal members. The number is not fixed by law, since it depends upon the nature and importance of the Congregation, and upon the free choice of the Roman Pontiff.[3] This body examines and settles more serious matters, and makes the more important decisions of the Congregation.[4]

Juridically the Congregation for the Propagation of the Faith consists of the cardinal members alone, for only they have a de-

---

[1] *Guida delle missioni cattoliche redacta sotto gli auspici della Sacra Congregazione de Prop. Fide* (Romae, 1934), p. 32 (hereafter referred to as *Guida*); *Normae peculiares*, cap. VII, art. VI, nn. 1-5—*AAS*, I (1909), 97-98 —*Fontes*, n. 6460.

[2] *Guida, loc. cit.*

[3] Stanghetti, *Prassi*, p. 99. Cf. Wernz-Vidal, *Ius Canonicum*, Vol. II, n. 483, where it is also stated that Sixtus V in 1588 had assigned five cardinals to each Congregation, except the Congregation of the Inquisition, which had seven. Monin, *De Curia Romana*, p. 196; *Normae communes*, cap. II, n. 1—*AAS*, 1 (1909), 37.

[4] *Normae peculiares*, cap. II, n. 1—*AAS*, I (1909), 61-62; De Meester, *op. cit.*, II, n. 581; Maroto, *Institutiones*, II, 246-247.

liberative voice at the meetings. Even their deliberative power, however, is always subordinated to the approval of the Supreme Pontiff, to whom the decisions of the *plenus Conventus* must be submitted.[5]

(1) The Cardinal Prefect: One of the cardinals is nominated by the Pope as Prefect,[6] to take care of the practical operation of the Congregation and assume the full responsibility for it. He presides at the *plenus Conventus* and also at the fiscal *Congressus* which performs the function of the former Prefect for fiscal matters (*Praefectus rei oeconomicae curandae*), and at the weekly *Congressus*.[7] Besides the performance of his ordinary functions in the Congregation, the Prefect enjoys substantial personal faculties.[8] Usually the Cardinal Prefect is also appointed by the Roman Pontiff as a member of other dicasteries which are related to the Congregation for the Propagation of the Faith (Holy Office, Consistorial Congregation, Congregation for the Oriental Church, Congregation for the Extraordinary Ecclesiastical Affairs, etc.). He is also the Grand Chancellor of the Pontifical University "*De Propaganda Fide.*"[9]

(2) The Major Officials: To the cardinalitial body forming the Congregation proper are attached two Prelates, as Secretary and Undersecretary.[10] These two major officials, like the cardinal members, are appointed by the Roman Pontiff. The Secretary directs the secretariat, the administration, the missionary works (he has the presidency of the Pontifical University "*De Propaganda Fide,*" and is Rector Magnificus of it and of the missionary Institute), in a word, all the offices and dependencies of

[5] Monin, *De Curia Romana,* p. 196: "Ipsi soli votum habent regulariter decisivum, ac proinde ipsis solis iuridice constant Congregationes." Cf. *Guida,* p. 32; Stanghetti, *Prassi,* p. 99; Coronata, *Institutiones Iuris Canonici,* I, 408.

[6] *Normae peculiares,* cap. VII, art. IV, n. 1—*AAS,* I (1909), 85; Badii, *Institutiones Iuris Canonici* (Florentiae, 1921), p. 173, n. 184.

[7] *Guida,* p. 33; Baart, *The Roman Court,* p. 222.

[8] *Normae peculiares,* cap. VII, art. III, n. 12—*AAS,* I (1909), 89.

[9] Stanghetti, *Prassi,* p. 99; Maroto, *Institutiones,* II, 238, 242.

[10] Ojetti, *De Romana Curia,* p. 110.

the Congregation.[11]   The Secretary has special duties in the internal administration of the Congregation. He attends the *plenus Conventus*, although without the right to vote; he participates in the fiscal *Congressus*, together with the Prosecretary of the fiscal department, as well as in the *Congressus* which the Secretary and the *minutanti* also attend.[12]

The matters discussed at the *plenus Conventus* include the erection of mission territories, various business affecting missions, changes from simple mission to apostolic prefecture, from apostolic prefecture to apostolic vicariate, nomination of ordinaries vested with episcopal character, approval of religious institutes of pontifical right, and the constitutions of such institutes, questions of a juridical nature, and so on.[13]

(3) The Consultors: There are also a number of consultors of the Congregation. Their opinion is solicited in more difficult questions. They do not meet *collegialiter*, except for those who belong to the Commission for Seminaries and Synods.[14] These assistants are appointed by the Roman Pontiff and are taken from the secular clergy and from religious and missionary institutes. They are selected for their competence in problems of an ecclesiastical and missionary nature.[15]

(4) The Minor Officials: The Congregation for the Propagation of the Faith includes minor officials such as *minutanti* (*studii adiutores seu informatores*),[16] archivists, protocolists, and clerks, who are selected by the *Congressus*, with the approval of the pope.[17]

---

[11] Stanghetti, *Prassi,* p. 102.

[12] *Guida,* p. 33.

[13] *Normae peculiares,* cap. II, n. 1—*AAS,* I (1909), 61-62.

[14] *Normae peculiares,* cap. VI, n. 1—*AAS,* I (1909), 70; Stanghetti, *Prassi,* pp. 103-104.

[15] *Guida,* p. 33; *Normae peculiares,* cap. VI, n. 1; cap. VII, art. III, n. 2—*AAS,* I (1909), 85; Cappello, *De Curia Romana,* I, 178; Ojetti, *De Romana Curia,* p. 70.

[16] Cf. Maroto, *Institutiones,* II, 240, footnote n. 1. Their functions are described in the *Normae peculiares,* cap. VI, nn. 3-5—*AAS,* I (1909), 71-73.

[17] *Normae peculiares,* cap. II, nn. 2-11—*AAS,* I (1909), 37-40; Ojetti, *op. cit.,* pp. xlv-xlvi. Cf. also Wernz-Vidal, *Ius Canonicum,* Vol. II, n. 483.

The duties of the *minutanti* are distributed in this manner: (a) *minutanti* for the mission territories of Northern and Southern Europe; of North, Central and South America; for religious institutes, and congregations of pontifical right; for missionary colleges; (b) *minutanti* for missions of Japan, Korea, Indochina, and Australasia; (c) *minutanti* for missions of India, Australia, and Oceania; (d) *minutanti* for missions of North and Central Africa; (e) *minutanti* for missions of China; (f) *minutanti* for the missions of South Africa, missionary works, and various other matters.[18]

The duties of the protocolists are to number and register documents according to the date of their arrival and to affix the outgoing date to other documents. Two employees are attached to this office.[19] Even today the duties of the clerks are not merely mechanical. They must make an accurate and suitable transcription of documents, although they do not have right to change the text. The mailing employees are in charge of summarizing in a register the contents of bulls and apostolic briefs which are processed through the Congregation for the Propagation of the Faith.[20]

The archivist must not only keep the archives in good order and in his custody, but he must also perform the necessary research, and supply to the superiors, the *minutanti* and possibly to authorized outsiders, the historical material for their respective study. Furthermore, he authenticates copies of the documents

---

There are also *apparitores* known as *deservientes* who make up the staff of servants, custodians and janitors. Cf. Maroto, *op. cit.,* p. 243; *Normae communes,* cap. II, n. 12—*AAS,* I (1909), 77.

[18] Stanghetti, *Prassi,* p. 105. Already at the times which immediately preceded the foundation of the Congregation, P. Tommasco di Gesù (1564-1627) while planning its constitution, wrote: "Hujus Congregationis quattuor aut quinque esse possent secretarii idonei, vel rerum et linguarum usu vel doctrina, vel, quod caput est, pietatis affectu praestantes; quorum munus esset cuncta ordine Congregationi proponere, constituta exsequi, orthodoxos et pios libellos pro ratione uniuscuiusque provinciae, variis linguis conscriptos habere, regesta literarum . . . asservare." Thomas a Iesu, *De Procuranda Salute* (Romae, 1940), p. 166.

[19] Stanghetti, *Prassi,* p. 105.

[20] *Ibid.,* p. 106; *Normae peculiares,* cap. VI, n. 6—*AAS,* I (1909), 73-74.

to be released, publishes the official notes of the Congregation for the Propagation of the Faith,[21] and reviews communications of the international agency *Fides*.[22]

A *schedarista* (note-writer) is entrusted with the task of examining each document, reporting the matters contained in them in suitable notes and thus constituting a third index (in addition to the protocol and the mailing lists). Another employee takes care of the restoration of ancient documents.[23]

Article 2. Administration of Temporalities

Originally, there were two Prefects of the Congregation for the Propagation of the Faith, each a Cardinal. One was the Prefect General, the other Prefect for fiscal matters. Under the constitution *Sapienti consilio* this latter office ceased and the entire administration of property was assigned to the Congregation itself.[24] The deliberative powers, the supreme direction, and the handling of affairs pertain to the *plenus Conventus*, a part of which (the Cardinal Prefect and two cardinal members) meets with the fiscal *Congressus* for the revision and approval of the annual financial statements and to deal with questions of particular importance. The administration prepares the reports for the fiscal *Congressus* and audits the documents in regard to the matters under discussion.[25]

The Prefect with major officials constitutes the *Congressus*.[26] The *Congressus*, however, is a consultive and executive body, and recourse may always be made to the *plenus Conventus* for more important matters.[27]

[21] *Loc. cit.*

[22] *Infra*, p. 44.

[23] *Loc. cit.*

[24] M. Martin, *The Roman Curia*, p. 74: "Praefectura specialis pro re oeconomica esse desinit; omnium vero bonorum additio, etiam Reverendae Camerae Spoliorum, ipsi Congregationi de Propaganda Fide committitur."; Pius X, const. *Sapienti consilio*, 29 iun. 1908—*AAS*, I (1909), 13; Cappello, *De Curia Romana*, I, 234; Prümmer, *Manuale Iuris Canonici* (Friburgi Brisgoviae, 1927), p. 143.

[25] Stanghetti, *Prassi*, pp. 107-108.

[26] *Normae communes*, cap. I, n. 3—*AAS*, I (1909), 37.

[27] De Meester, *op. cit.*, II, 70, footnotes nn. 6, 8.

The Prosecretary of the fiscal department, who depends directly upon the Cardinal Prefect and Secretary, is the head of the temporal administration. He has the responsibility for all the temporal functions of the Congregation for the Propagation of the Faith and its dependent bodies. The Prosecretary is named by the Roman Pontiff. He participates in the fiscal *Congressus* of the Congregation and is also a member of the fiscal Board of the Pontifical University *"De Propaganda Fide."* [28]

The personnel of the temporal administration is almost entirely composed of laymen:

(1) The first section (accounting and cash) comprises the chief accountant, an assistant accountant, and six bookkeepers, among whom the various duties are distributed (journal, administration of the fixed assets, securities and bank operations, pension fund, billing, etc.). There are also a cashier and two collectors.[29]

(2) The second section (secretariat) consists of two *minutanti* for the study of fiscal administrative matters, an archivist, and a mailing clerk.[30]

(3) There is finally a third section (technical and legal), which comprises at present a consultant, a procurator, a notary, an archivist, an agronomist, and a land-superintendent.

To the administration are added the management of *l'Azienda Spogli* (concerned with the vacant benefices of the old pontifical State), the Monte Carafa, the Pontifical University *"De Propaganda Fide,"* and various estates.[31]

Article 3. Special Organizations in the Congregation

Among the instruments of the Congregation are various works and pious unions which collect the material means for the development of the missionary activity of the Church. There are three especially important pontifical organizations to be considered, although the Code does not say anything concerning them.

(1) The Pontifical Society for the Propagation of the Faith:

[28] Stanghetti, *Prassi*, p. 108.

[29] *Loc. cit.*

[30] *Loc. cit.*

[31] *Guida*, p. 32; Stanghetti, *Prassi*, pp. 108-109.

This has the specific purpose of collecting funds throughout the world and of promoting prayers for the missions.[32] Founded in Lyons in 1820 at the initiative of Pauline Jaricot and organized in 1822, it spread throughout France, Italy, Belgium, Switzerland, Germany, Spain, Ireland, England, and the United States of America. Until 1922, this society kept its private and mostly national character. On the occasion of its first centennial, the organization was made pontifical and international. The chief office was transferred from Lyons to Rome, near the Congregation for the Propagation of the Faith, where it still is.[33]

At the head of the work is placed a General Superior Council, formed of members elected from the clergy of the nations which are most deserving in this matter. This council is presided over by the Secretary of the Congregation. The office of Vice-president is reserved to a director from France, in due consideration of the merits of this nation in the work of the society. The General Superior Council annually (usually in the month of March) distributes funds to the various mission countries, according to the directions given by the Congregation itself.

In the individual countries there are national councils, whose presidents are named by the Congregation. In the individual dioceses, the bishops appoint diocesan directors. A special activity of this pontifical work of great interest is the international agency *Fides*, instituted in 1927 with the purpose of collecting data concerning missionary circumstances. This depends directly upon the General Superior Council. In 1939, a statistical department was added to the agency. This is constantly kept informed with data supplied directly by the heads of the missions and the missionaries themselves.[34]

[32] Pius XI, motu propr. *Romanorum pontificum*, 3 maii 1922—*AAS*, XIV (1922), 324: ". . . instrumentum ad fidelium stipes undique cogendas easque erogandas."

[33] Hickey, *The Society for the Propagation of the Faith, Its Foundation, Organization and Success* (1822-1922), The Catholic University of America Studies in American Church History, Vol. III (Washington, D. C.: The Catholic University of America Press, 1922), pp. 10-47; Pius XI, motu propr. *Romanorum pontificum*, 3 maii 1922—*AAS*, XIV (1922), 321-330.

[34] Stanghetti, *Prassi*, pp. 87-88; Testore, "Agenzia Internationale Fides,"

(2) The Pontifical Association of St. Peter the Apostle for the Native Clergy has the special purpose of helping in the education of native clergy in the mission countries. It originated in France at the initiative of Stéphanie Bigard and upon the suggestion of Bishop Cousin, Vicar Apostolic of Nagasaki, Japan, in 1889. It was blessed by Leo XIII in 1895, approved by the Bishop of Seez, France, in 1895, and encouraged by the Congregation for the Propagation of the Faith in 1896. In 1902 the organization was recognized as a civil moral person in Switzerland, where the chief office was established in Freiburg. At the death of Stéphanie Bigard in 1904, the work was entrusted to the Franciscan Missionaries of Mary, until the Congregation provisionally approved its statutes by a decree of April 28, 1920. Finally, the organization was accepted as pontifical by two papal documents of June 24, 1929. The chief office is now located near the Congregation.[35]

At the head of this work is a General Council with general offices in Rome, presided over by the Secretary of the Congregation for the Propagation of the Faith. There are national councils and in the dioceses diocesan directors.[36]

(3) In 1843 the Pontifical Association of the Holy Childhood was founded by Bishop Janson of Nancy, France, for the purpose of collecting alms from Catholic children in order to rescue and baptize abandoned Chinese children. Soon the idea of this organization was expanded to include the Christian education of children, not only from China, but from the whole infidel world. It later established orphanages, refuges, schools, and laboratories in various missions. The work had the approval of the Holy See, from a brief of Gregory XVI on July 18, 1846, but only with

---

Enciclopedia Cattolica (1948), I, 447; Pius XI, motu propr. *Romanorum pontificum*, 3 maii 1922—*AAS*, XIV (1922), 328-330.

[35] Stanghetti, *Prassi*, p. 88; Pius XI, motu propr. *Vix ad Summi*, 24 iun. 1929—*AAS*, XXI (1929), 347, ad II: "A christifidelibus preces piaque opera eo consilio postulet, ut caelestis pastorum Princeps quam plurimos velit ex ethnicis nationibus iuvenes bene animatos superno quodam instincto ad sacerdotium vocare, itemque velit quos sua adspirante gratia ad huiusmodi inceptum sanctissimum allexerit, iidem scientia ac virtute praestantes omnino evadant."

[36] Stanghetti, *Prassi*, pp. 88-89.

the motu proprio *Romanorum Pontificum* of 1922 was it recognized as pontifical. The chief office is still located in Paris.[37]

Upon the central council of this organization depend the national councils and upon the latter the diocesan councils. In each parish, the parish priest is the director of the work, which is regularly constituted as soon as twelve members are gathered. No special formalities are required for its establishment in a parish.[38]

On June 24, 1929, Pius XI issued the *motu proprio Decessor noster* to determine the relations between the Pontifical Society for the Propagation of the Faith and the Pontifical Association of St. Peter the Apostle for the Native Clergy. These are the main stipulations or interrelations: (a) the Secretary of the Congregation for the Propagation of the Faith is the President of both pontifical Works; (b) the Secretary General of the Pontifical Society for the Propagation of the Faith is a member of the General Council of the Pontifical Association of St. Peter the Apostle for the Native Clergy; and likewise, the Secretary General of the Pontifical Association of St. Peter the Apostle is a member of the General Council of the Pontifical Society for the Propagation of the Faith; (c) a Supreme Committee, consisting of the President, the General Secretaries of both pontifical Works, and a councillor from each, chosen by his council, provides for the cooperation of the respective activities; (d) these pontifical Works (including the Pontifical Association of the Holy Childhood) are directly subject to the jurisdiction of the Congregation for the Propagation of the Faith.[39]

The above mentioned three pontifical Works are not a part of the *instituta ecclesiastica*, since they lack the character of foundation, with endowment of goods, in permanent form, etc., which are spoken of in Canon 1490.[40] Instead, the three pontifi-

[37] Cf. Pius XI, motu propr. *Romanorum pontificum*, 3 maii 1922—*AAS*, XIV (1922), 326; Pius XI, ep. encycl. *Rerum ecclesiae*, 28 febr. 1926—*AAS*, XVIII (1926), 72; Pius XI, motu propr. *Decessor noster*, 24 iun. 1929—*AAS*, XXI (1929), 346.

[38] Stanghetti, *Prassi, loc. cit.*

[39] Pius XI, motu propr. *Decessor noster*, 24 iun. 1929—*AAS*, XXI (1929), 343-344.

[40] Cf. can. 1489-1497.

cal Works are associations of members of the Church and chiefly of lay people. They are, thus, included in the *associationes fidelium.*[41]

In general, the rules which canonically govern these associations are determined by their status as voluntary societies of the faithful, founded or at least approved [42] by the ecclesiastical authorities, for the performance of a pious or charitable work, *"ad aliqua pietatis aut caritatis opera exercenda,"* without common life.[43]

These lay associations are distinct from religious institutes.[44] They are moral persons and therefore have perpetuity [45] as well as the right to acquire, receive, and administer temporal goods.[46] They have the *ius standi in iudicio* before the ecclesiastical courts.[47] As the purpose of the three pontifical Works is not of merely private interest, but looks to the missionary activity of the universal Church, they must be considered public persons.[48]

---

[41] Cf. can. 684, 686. This section of Book II of the Code of Canon Law, which contains these canons, concerns the laity. Clerics may of course be members of such associations but this does not change their character.

[42] A distinction must be made between recommendation, approval and establishment. Cf. Cappello, *Summa Iuris Canonici* (3 vols., Romae, 1939), II, 281; Romani, *Institutiones Iuris Canonici* (2 vols. in 3, Romae, 1941-1945), I, 430: " Approbatio est actus ecclesiasticae potestatis, quo associatio agnoscitur qua talis certisque donatur favoribus tutelaque iuris; erectio autem est actus potestatis ecclesiasticae, quo associatio . . . constituitur in personam moralem canonicam"; Vromant, *De Fidelium Associationibus* (Louvain, 1932), p. 6: "Associationes ab ecclesia mere commendatae constituuntur a privatis; non sunt uniones vere ecclesiasticae, dominii ecclesiastici non sunt capaces, neque, qua tales pro suo speciali fine Ordinariis locorum subduntur."

[43] Can. 685.

[44] Can. 487-681.

[45] Can. 102.

[46] Can. 1495, § 2.

[47] Can. 1557, § 2, n. 2; 1649.

[48] One should keep in mind the criteria for the distinction between public legal persons and private legal persons, thus enumerated by La Torre: (a) the collective aim (not limited to a small number of individuals); (b) the recognition by statute as a public person (not as a simple moral person);

These organizations have their own statutes, and have been duly constituted by the Holy See. It seems that they enjoy the privilege of not being subjected, in the strict sense, to the jurisdiction of the ordinaries with regard to the *ius cognoscendi* and the *ius prescribendi*.[49] Their supervision by the Congregation for the Propagation of the Faith encompassed the administration of money received, the distribution of the funds to the various mission countries and the various institutes, the nomination of the national directors, the communication of instructions, and, in some circumstances, the solution of doubts and the settlement of disputes which possibly may arise within the pontifical Works, or between the pontifical Works, or between them and others.[50] Any lawful members [51] enjoy the rights, privileges, indulgences, and spiritual favors granted to the pontifical Works themselves, unless they have been legally expelled.[52] One ceases to be a member upon either expulsion or acceptance of resignation, but the privileges, etc., cease *ipso facto*, if the prescribed conditions are not fulfilled.[53] Finally, the pontifical Works may be canonically suppressed only by the Holy See.[54]

(4) Besides the three pontifical Works, there is the Pious Missionary Union for the Clergy.[55] It is simply an association of priests and clerics which pursues the diffusion of the missionary idea among the clergy, and through this means, among the faithful.

(c) the power to command (less in pious societies); (d) subjection to the direct supervision of the State, or Chancery, etc.—La Torre, *Nozione di dir. amministrativo* (Romae, 1935), p. 30.

49 Can. 690.

50 Stanghetti, *Prassi*, p. 95.

51 Can. 692; cf. can. 693, § 3; Vromant, *op. cit.*, p. 37, footnote n. 3— Some exceptions are made, e.g., in the case of the pontifical association of the Holy Childhood, as the members are children.

52 S.C.P.F., decl. *Plurimi*, 1 febr. 1928—*AAS*, XX (1928), 190-210. Normally, the conditions of canon 692 are required, but this is not necessary in the case of the Pontifical Society for the Propagation of the Faith.

53 Can. 72, § 1.

54 Can. 699, § 2: "Associationes ab ipsa Apostolica Sede erectae nonisi ab eadem supprimi possunt."

55 Benedict XV, ep. ap. *Maximum illud*, 30 nov. 1919; *Sylloge*, p. 676.

This union was founded by Father Paolo Mana, Superior of the Pontifical Institute of the Foreign Missions in Milan. It received pontifical approval on October 31, 1916. Later, on April 4, 1926, it obtained approval for its statutes from the Congregation for the Propagation of the Faith. This organization does not have the same characteristics as those of the three pontifical Works, since it does not collect offerings.[56]

When the statutes of the Missionary Union for the Clergy were revised in April, 1937, the Congregation for the Propagation of the Faith wrote to all ordinaries to stress the urgency of founding the Union everywhere:

> This is why it seems to us that the Missionary Union for the Clergy, if it is used successfully, can serve advantageously as the basis for the expansion of the missions. Consequently let it be given new vigor in every diocese of the Catholic world; where by chance it does not exist, let it be founded without delay. Thus neither workers, nor resources, nor the support of prayers will be lacking to the growing expansion of the Church.[57]

Besides the Missionary Union for the Clergy, the following deserve mention:

(a) The Work for the Negroes of Africa (*opus pro nigritis Africae*), instituted by Leo XIII in the encyclical *Catholicae ecclesiae* of November 20, 1890, to collect money each year on the feast of the Epiphany. This organization is not pontifical. Its direction pertains to the Cardinal Prefect of the Congregation for the Propagation of the Faith.[58]

(b) The Apostolic Work, founded by Maria Du Chesne in France in 1838, which has the aim of providing sacred furnishings for the churches of the missions, clothing for the missionaries, neophytes, and catechumens. Central office is in Paris.[59]

---

[56] S.C.P.F., decr. *Ut pia,* 4 apr. 1926—*AAS,* XVIII (1926), 231; S.C.P.F., decr. *Piae unionis,* 14 apr. 1937—*AAS,* XXIX (1937), 435.

[57] S.C.P.F., decr. *Piae unionis,* 14 apr. 1937—*AAS,* XXIX (1937), 435-441; S.C.P.F., instr. *Ut universa,* 3 mart. 1937—*AAS,* XXIX (1937), 476-477—*Sylloge,* pp. 702-703.

[58] Stanghetti, *Prassi,* p. 91.

[59] *Loc. cit.*

(c) The Sodality of St. Peter Claver, founded in 1894 by Countess M. Teresia Ledochowska at Salsburg, Austria, to aid African missions. It was approved by the Holy See in 1910. The sodality has as its nucleus a true religious congregation of women. The chief office is in Rome.[60]

(d) Various missionary associations for students, established since 1910 in various countries, for the purpose of spreading knowledge of the missions and encouraging missionary activity.[61]

(e) Furthermore, various works of a national, local, or private nature (some of them instituted by religious congregations) which exist in many countries.[62]

ARTICLE 4. NATURE AND EXERCISE OF POWER

What is the nature of the jurisdiction imparted to the Congregation for the Propagation of the Faith? It is obviously an ordinary power, for it is attached to the Congregation by law.[63] This ordinary power is vicarious, because it is exercised in the name of the Roman Pontiff.[64] It is, moreover, an administrative power and not a judicial one, since the Code attributes contentious jurisdiction to the tribunals, as Pius X states in his constitution *Sapienti consilio:*

> The Sacred Congregations no longer receive or hear contentious cases, civil or criminal, requiring the judiciary order with a process and proofs.[65]

To what extent is the Congregation for the Propagation of the Faith obliged to have its actions sanctioned by the Roman Pon-

[60] Can. 702, § 1: "Associationes fidelium . . . si ad modum organici corporis sint constitutae, sodalitia audiunt." Hilgers, "Sodality," *The Catholic Encyclopedia,* IV (1912), 126.

[61] Hilgers, *loc. cit.*

[62] Champagne, *Manual of Missionary Action* (Ottawa: University of Ottawa, 1948), pp. 455–456; cf. *Guida,* p. 516.

[63] Can. 197, § 1; cf. can. 145; 252.

[64] Can. 197, § 2. The power does not cease at the death of the Pope, but it must not be exercised, then, except for granting favors of lesser importance.

[65] Pius X, const. *Sapienti consilio,* 29 iun. 1908—*AAS,* I (1909), 18—*Fontes,* n. 682.

tiff himself? There are some authors who deny that the Roman Congregations possess true legislative power. The law of the Code in accordance with the law of the constitution *Sapienti consilio* establishes a general principle, namely, *nihil grave et extraordinarium* may be considered by the Congregations, before the matter has been communicated to the Roman Pontiff, who reserves to himself the approval of the favors granted and the resolutions adopted by the dicasteries.[66] According to the opinions of Wernz-Vidal,[67] Cappello,[68] Monin,[69] and Jone,[70] universal laws are always grave and extraordinary. Therefore, they are so much beyond the power of the Congregations that the latter cannot be said to have legislative power.

Does the Congregation for the Propagation of the Faith have the authority to issue new laws concerning the mission territories? It should be noted that nowhere does the Code expressly mention any legislative power of the Roman Congregations. Since the constitution *Sapienti consilio* was issued, it would seem that the Congregation for the Propagation of the Faith has no legislative power in the proper sense, unless it possesses a mandate from the Roman Pontiff. A further reason for denying legislative power to the Congregations is to be found in the *motu proprio Cum iuris* of September 15, 1917.[71] By this document Benedict XV established the Commission for the Authentic Interpretation of the Code, and also laid down the following important norms to be observed in this matter:

> The Sacred Roman Congregations should not henceforth issue *new General Decrees*, unless some grave necessity of the universal Church urges otherwise. Their ordinary duty,

[66] Can. 244; Pius X, const. *Sapienti consilio*, 29 iun. 1908—*AAS*, I (1909), 18—*Fontes*, n. 682. Cf. Sixtus V, const. *Immensa aeterni Dei*, 22 ian. 1588 —*Bull. Rom.*, VIII, 985-999.

[67] *Ius Canonicum*, II, 566.

[68] *De Curia Romana* (2 vols., Romae, 1911-1912), I, 42.

[69] *De Curia Romana*, p. 216.

[70] *Commentarium in Codicem Iuris Canonici* (Paderborn: Schoningh, 1950), I, 235.

[71] Benedict XV, motu propr. *Cum iuris*, 15 sept. 1917—*AAS*, IX (1917), 483-484.

> therefore, in this matter will be to urge the faithful to the
> observance of the Code and, if there is occasion, to issue
> *Instructions* by which the prescriptions of the Code are ex-
> plained and their observance is made effective. . . . If, in
> the course of time, the good of the universal Church shall
> require that a new general decree be issued by any Sacred
> Congregation, the Sacred Congregation itself shall issue the
> decree and if it disagrees with the prescriptions of the Code,
> the Sacred Congregation should inform the Supreme Pon-
> tiff of such discrepancy. . . . [72]

The above mentioned general decrees are true laws; the *motu
proprio* indicates carefully the way in which they are to be in-
serted in the Code.   From this it may be argued that the power
to make these laws is beyond the competence of the Congregations; therefore, the latter do not enjoy true legislative power.[73]

On the other hand, there are those who would attribute true
legislative power to the Roman Congregations.   Sipos,[74] Cicognani,[75] Maroto,[76] Coronata,[77] Michiels,[78] Vermeersch-Creusen,[79]

---

[72] Sacrae Romanae Congregationes nova Decreta Generalia iamnunc ne
ferant, nisi qua gravis Ecclesiae universae necessitas aliud suadeat.   Ordinarium igitur earum munus in hoc genere erit tum curare ut Codicis
praescripta religiose serventur, tum Instructiones, si ferat, edere, quae
iisdem Codicis praescriptis maiorem et lucem afferant et efficientiam pari-
ant. Si quando, decursu temporum, Ecclesiae universae bonum postulabit,
ut novum generale decretum ab aliqua Sacra Congregatione condatur,
ea ipsa decretum conficiat, quod si a Codicis praescriptis dissentiat, Sum-
mum Pontificem de eiusmodi discrepantia moneat. . . .   Cf. McManus,
The Congregation of Sacred Rites, The Catholic University of America
Canon Law Studies, n. 352 (Washington, D. C.: The Catholic University
of America Press, 1954), p. 49.   The material in Article IV is drawn
principally from McManus, *The Congregation of Sacred Rites*, pp. 49-53.

[73] In the passage following the one quoted above.

[74] *Enchiridion Iuris Canonici*, p. 206.

[75] *Canon Law* (2. ed., Reprint; Westminster, Maryland: Newman, 1949),
p. 78.

[76] *Institutiones*, I, 411.

[77] *Institutiones Iuris Canonici*, I, 399.

[78] *Normae Generales*, I, 219.

[79] *Epitome Iuris Canonici*, I, 304.

and Van Hove [80] claim that the Congregations have some legislative power. This, according to Van Hove, is the more common opinion of canonists.[81]

The *motu proprio* certainly confirms this position, since it allows such decrees when the serious need of the Church requires them and, thus, confirms the legislative power to be exercised, even though it is under certain limited circumstances.

If one were to accept the position of those who assert the necessity of papal approval *in forma specifica* for the general decrees, then the distinction between approval *in forma communi* and *in forma specifica* would be meaningless. The terms used in a general manner *in forma communi* are the following: *Facto verbo cum Sanctissimo, Ex audientia Sanctissimi, Probante Sanctissimo Domino, In solita audientia. . . . Sanctitas Sua resolutionem approbavit et confirmavit.*[82] Such a decree, issued with this kind of papal approval, remains an act of the respective Congregation, not pontifical law, which therefore possesses true legislative power. There seems to be no reason to require papal approval in forma specifica. The motu proprio of Benedict XV or Canon 244 make no specific mention of such an approval.[83] The *forma specifica*, on the other hand, is expressed usually in these terms: *Motu proprio, Ex certa scientia, De apostolicae auctoritatis plenitudine.*[84] In this case, the law or decree becomes true pontifical law.

Pius X indicated additional reasons favoring true legislative power for the Congregations, when he decreed the promulgation of laws in the *Acta Apostolicae Sedis*. He specifically mentioned the work of the Congregations *ad leges iam latas declarandas aut*

---

[80] *Commentarium Lovaniense in Codicem Iuris Canonici,* Vol. I, Tom. I, *Prolegomena* (2. ed., Mechliniae, Romae: Dessain, 1945), p. 74.

[81] *Loc. cit.*

[82] Cf. Regatillo, *Institutiones Iuris Canonici,* I, 305; cf. can. 291, § 1.

[83] Coronata, *Institutiones Iuris Canonici,* I, 406.

[84] Cicognani, *Canon Law,* p. 80; Chelodi, *Ius Canonicum de Personis,* p. 256; Sipos, *op. cit.,* p. 204; Regatillo, *op. cit.,* I, 291; Cance, *Le Code de Droit Canonique* (3 vols., Paris, 1927-1929), I, 249-250.

ad novas constituendas.[85]   Moreover, in the *Normae peculiares* issued at the same time the procedure was determined for legislation by the Congregations.[86]

What valid conclusions may be offered? The Congregation for the Propagation of the Faith has true legislative power, although it is restricted in its exercise. Indeed, this true legislative power is applicable only when some great need of the missions requires its formal application. If any new general decree is not in accord with the Code, the Roman Pontiff is informed of the discrepancy. If any new general decree is outside the ambit of the Code, then the general principle of Canon 244 obtains, thus reserving exclusively to the Roman Pontiff inspection and decision of grave and extraordinary affairs prior to the examination and solution of the respective Congregation for the Propagation of the Faith.[87]

Also, in each case, no new law of any importance may be enacted without the direct intervention of the Roman Pontiff. The general principle of Canon 244 and the constant practice of the Congregation point up the wisdom of pursuing this mode of action.[88]

Moreover, for the sake of efficiency, the Congregation for the Propagation of the Faith keeps a close check on all prescriptions of the Code concerning its functions. Whenever the occasion requires clarifying instructions of enactments, the Congregation issues instructions as explanatory and complementary to the Code. These instructions are not laws in the strict sense, nor an exercise of legislative power.[89]

[85] Const. *Promulgandi,* 29 sept. 1908—*AAS,* I (1909), 1.

[86] *Normae peculiares,* cap. II, n. 1—*Fontes,* n. 6460. Cf. Coronata, *op. cit.,* I, 399.

[87] Grentrup, *Ius Missionum,* p. 33; Benedict XV, motu propr. *Cum iuris,* 15 sept. 1917—*AAS,* IX (1917), 483-484.

[88] Grentrup, *loc. cit.*

[89] S.C.P.F., instr. *Quum huic,* 8 dec. 1929—*AAS,* XXII (1930), 111-115; *AAS,* IX (1917), 483-484.

CHAPTER IV

THE ROMAN PONTIFF AND THE PRESENT DIRECT COMPETENCE OF THE CONGREGATION SINCE THE CODE OF CANON LAW

ARTICLE 1. ROMAN PONTIFF

Dogmatically and canonically, the Roman Pontiff is the first and highest possessor of the right and duty imposed by God to spread the faith.[1] The Roman Pontiff as the supreme shepherd of the Church and as the supervisor of the Congregation for the Propagation of the Faith, as well as of the other Roman Congregations, possesses supreme power over all the missions and all the missionary activities of the Church. This power is truly episcopal, ordinary, and immediate, over all the churches severally and individually, over all the pastors, priests, and faithful together, and over each one of them.[2]

The Roman Pontiff is naturally free to involve himself directly in missionary problems but is not obliged to occupy himself personally with every missionary concern. Often the pope acts through the intermediary of the Secretariat of State in matters affecting the missions. Nevertheless, the established missionary agencies employed by the pope are the various Roman Congregations which are directly or indirectly competent in mission matters, and principally the Congregation for the Propagation of the Faith.[3]

From the Roman Pontiff come the powers of the Congregation for the Propagation of the Faith, whose decrees for this reason

---

[1] *Guida,* p. 30; can. 1350, § 2.

[2] Can. 218, §§ 1, 2. The doctrine of this canon was solemnly stated by the Vatican Council, Session IV, ch. III, de vi et ratione primatus Romani Pontificis. Denzinger, *Enchiridion Symbolorum, Definitionum, et Declarationum de Rebus Fidei et Morum* (Friburgi Brisgoviae: Herder, 1947), nn. 1670-1677.

[3] *Guida,* p. 30; Champagne, *Manual of Missionary Action,* p. 65.

contain the clause: *"vi facultatum a Ssmo Domino Nostro tribu-
tarum,"* or similar expressions. This pontifical sanction is given
at ordinary or scheduled audiences, or else at extraordinary audiences, all granted by the Roman Pontiff to the Cardinal Prefect, the Secretary, or, under unusual circumstances, to the Subsecretary of the Congregation.[4] In mission territories, pontifical
jurisdiction is in fact the only jurisdiction which is exercised.
The Code reserves to the Roman Pontiff the organization and the
care of the missions. Canon 1350, § 2, which reserves to the
Apostolic See the exclusive direction of missionary activity, does
not establish a new right;[5] it merely defines as explicitly entrusted a special authority exercised for many centuries.

In the exercise of jurisdiction in mission regions, the Roman
Pontiff is not restricted by any territorial limit. His jurisdiction
is exercised freely and independently in mission lands. In practice, however, this immediate authority is not exercised so freely
in all mission countries, since account must be taken of the concordats between the Apostolic See and various nations.[6] A re-
cent instance of such a concordat was the one entered into on
May 7, 1940, by the Apostolic See and the Republic of Portugal.[7]
This agreement climaxed efforts made for more than a century
by the Roman Pontiffs, especially Gregory XVI,[8] Pius IX,[9] and

---

[4] Stanghetti, *Prassi*, p. 99. The Cardinal Prefect has an ordinary audience with the Pope on the first and the third Thursday of each month; the
Secretary, on the second and fourth Tuesday.

[5] Can. 1350, § 2: "In aliis territoriis universa missionum cura apud acatholicos Sedi Apostolicae unice reservatur." Cf. *Coll. S.C.P.F.*, I, nn. 3, 9.

[6] Can. 3.

[7] Bouscaren, *The Canon Law Digest* (4 vols., Milwaukee: Bruce, 1933-
1957), II, 11-24 (hereafter referred as as *Digest*); *AAS*, XXXII (1940),
217-244. The Holy See may, upon agreement with the Government, modify
the number of the dioceses and missionary districts. The Holy See may
choose archbishops, bishops, etc., but before their appointment must communicate the name of the person chosen to the Portuguese Government.
New missionary boards of administration have to be directed by a Portuguese citizen, unless consultation with Portuguese Government precedes a
different disposition.

[8] In 1832, Gregory XVI had required the King of Portugal either to
honor his missionary commitments or to renounce the right of patronage.

Leo XIII.[10]

The principle of the proper, direct and universal competence of the Roman Pontiff over the missions was fully recognized internationally during the Peace conference after World War I in 1919. The allied powers agreed, at the urging of Msgr. Cerretti, a special delegate of Benedict XV, to re-word the articles 122 and 438 of the Versailles Treaty.[11] As a result, the replacement of the German missionaries in the former colonies of the German Empire was made with the respect to the traditional rights of the Apostolic See and with its consent.[12]

Missionaries activities are vast, as is evident from documents found in the *Acta Apostolic Sedis, Sylloge*, etc.[13] The Roman Pontiff cannot by himself perform all the functions of govern-

On April 24, 1838, the constitution *Multa praeclare,* of the same Pope, severely limited the rights of the patronage. The four dioceses of Cranganor, Cochin, Meliapour, and Malacca, were abolished and replaced by apostolic vicariates, while the jurisdiction of the archbishop of Goa was restricted exclusively to the territory subject to the dominion of Portugal. Cf. De Martinis, *Ius Pontificrum*, V, 195-198.

[9] The action of Gregory XVI provoked the most violent reaction from the Portuguese government and even caused a schism among the clergy of Goa. Pius IX, after vain attempts to restore order in India, concluded a concordat with Portugal in 1857. This reestablished, in large measure, the conditions prior to 1838. Cf. Grentrup, *op. cit.*, pp. 211-212.

[10] On August 7, 1886, a new agreement was contracted between Leo XIII and the government at Lisbon. The rights and interests of the Church were better protected, and additional concessions were granted in 1887 and 1890. Cf. Grentrup, *op. cit.*, pp. 213-214.

[11] Cf. *La Documentation Catholique* (Paris, 1919), pp. 194-196; Hayes-Baldwin-Cole, *History of Europe* (New York: Macmillan, 1955), pp. 922-924; McSorley, *An Outline History of the Church by Centuries* (St. Louis, Mo.: Herder, 1957), pp. 892, 988.

[12] Art. 122 required the expulsion of all German Catholic missionaries without giving any guarantee of the continuance of their work. Art. 438 made it possible that the property of the Catholic missions might pass into the hands of non-Catholics. A clause was, then, added to art. 122 by which the powers of the Entente committed themselves to safeguard the missions. Art. 438 was reworded so that the property of the Catholic missions would not be endangered. Cf. *La Documentation Catholique, loc. cit.*

[13] *AAS*, since its establishment in 1908; cf. also *Sylloge*, published in 1939, covering the missionary acts of the Apostolic See from 1907 to May 1937.

ment of the missions. He is in fact aided by the vicars and prefects apostolic and those who participate by ecclesiastical law in the power of the supreme pontificate, as well as by the cardinals and other officials of the Roman Congregations, in particular by the Congregation for the Propagation of the Faith.[14]

Article 2. Canon 252, § 1.

Canon 252, §1, is derived from the constitution *Inscrutabili* of June 22, 1622.[15] The duties and scope of powers of the Congregation for the Propagation of the Faith are delineated in this paragraph. According to the original text of the constitution *Inscrutabili*, the Congregation had very extensive authority, including jurisdiction over all matters pertaining to mission affairs throughout the world. The only exception was matters called *graviora*, which were to be referred to the Roman Pontiff. In the course of time, however, these vast powers became better defined in the Code of Canon Law.[16]

> Congregatio de Propaganda Fide missionibus ad praedicandum Evangelium et catholicam doctrinam praeest, ministros necessarios constituit et mutat, facultatemque habet tractandi, agendi et exsequendi omnia hac in re necessaria et opportuna.

A. *Meaning of Mission According to the Congregation*

Before approaching the question involved, it is necessary to define certain notions of "mission" according to its acceptance in Canon Law.

The word mission (Latin *missio,* from *mittere,* to send) is used

---

[14] *Reg.* 72, *R.J.,* in VI°; cf. also *reg.* 68, *R.J.,* in VI°: "Potest quis per alium, quod potest facere per seipsum."

[15] Gregory XV, const. *Inscrutabili,* 22 iun. 1622—*Coll. S.C.P.F.,* n. 3: "Missionibus omnibus ad praedicandum et docendum evangelium, et catholicam doctrinam superintendant, ministros necessarios constituant, et mutent. Nos enim eis. . . ."

[16] M. Martin, *The Roman Curia,* p. 61; Baart, *The Roman Court,* pp. 208-209; Hilling, "Die rechtliche Stellung der Propagandakongregation nach der neuen Kurialreform Pius X," *Zeitschrift für Missionswissenschaft,* I (1911), 156.

in various ways. Mission can be considered in three ways, namely, the common, dogmatic, and juridical notions.[17]

Here, the consideration of this term is limited to the juridical notion only. Mission may be considered juridical in two ways: (a) In the broad sense, a mission is called canonical in Canon Law [18] which is an act of legitimate authority deputizing someone to exercise jurisdiction.[19] An application of this principle is used in regard to preaching for which, according to Canon 1328, a mission from the legitimate ecclesiastical authority is required. The canonical mission to preach, then, may be defined as a positive deputation by the competent ecclesiastical authority to teach the Christian faith officially and in a public manner.[20] (b) In the strict sense, a distinction in the meaning of mission should be made between home (*internal*) mission [21] and foreign (*external*) mission.[22] These notions will be discussed later in Article 1, C of Chapter V.

Here, in Canon 252, § 1, and according to the mission law, the term *missiones* refers to mission territory. Such territory is coextensive with the jurisdiction of the Congregation for the Propagation of the Faith, and consequently the meaning of mission according to the usage of this Congregation connotes the territory of the missions.[23] This is in accord with the original

[17] Sartori, *Iuris Missionarii Elementa* (Romae: Secretaria Missionum Ord. Fr. Minorum, 1947), p. 9; Paventi, *Breviarium Iuris Missionalis* (Romae: Catholic Book Agency, 1952), p. 9.

[18] Can. 109.

[19] Vromant, *Ius Missionariorum, Introductio et Normae Generales*, p. 1; Grentrup, *Ius Missionarium*, p. 1; Champagne, *Manual of Missionary Action*, p. 28.

[20] Regatillo, *Institutiones Iuris Canonici*, II, 87.

[21] Can. 1349, § 1.

[22] Can. 252, § 3; 1350, § 2.

[23] Grentrup, "Die Definition des Missionbegriffes," *Zeitschrift für Missionswissenschaft*, III (1913-1914), 265; *ibid.*, pp. 272-273: "Man könte namlich nur sagen: Kirchenrechtlich sind jene Gebiete als Missionen zu betrachten, die der Propagandakongregation unsterstellt sind." Cf. Paventi, *op. cit.*, p. 10.

text of the constitution *Inscrutabili,* "*missionibus omnibus ad praedicandum Evangelium. . . .*" [24]

Mission territory (*terra missionum*) may be considered under two aspects: (a) In the usual sense, mission territory refers to the planting of the faith only. In this sense, it is a territory in which the major part of the inhabitants has not yet been baptized, and is still outside the Church. From this point of view, all pagan lands are mission territories. The external criterion of this condition is the absence of the ecclesiastical hierarchy.[25] (b) In a scientific sense, namely, from the point of view of the consolidation of the faith, mission territory may be considered also as territory where the ordinary ecclesiastical hierarchy is established, but where it has not yet reached the organic and functional maturity which is characteristic of an adult Church.[26] These hierarchies still remain under the jurisdiction of the Congregation for the Propagation of the Faith, e.g., in Japan, China, Indo-China, Australia, East Indies, etc.[27]

The question may be raised whether the term mission territory may be used only for places under the Congregation for the Propagation of the Faith. In fact, the territories of the Latin Church under the jurisdiction of the Congregation for the Oriental Church and the Congregation for Extraordinary Ecclesiastical Affairs are also to be considered as mission areas.

(1) All the territories which pertain to the Congregation for the Propagation of the Faith by reason of the *status missionis* and which are subject to the Congregation by reason of the formative stage of the hierarchical development of the Church, are considered mission territories under the jurisdiction of this Congregation.[28] It should be added that the Congregation for the Propagation of the Faith considers as missions not only the

[24] Gregory XV, const. *Inscrutabili,* 22 iun. 1622—*Coll. S.C.P.F.,* I, n. 3; *Bull. S.C.P.F.,* I, 28; De Martinis, *Ius Pontificium,* I, 2.

[25] Sartori, *Iuris Missionarii Elementa,* p. 12.

[26] Sartori, *op. cit.,* pp. 12-13.

[27] Sartori, *op. cit.,* p. 13.

[28] S.C.P.F., decr. *Ordinarii,* 9 dec. 1920—*AAS,* XIII (1921), 17-18—*Sylloge,* n. 85: "Cum dioeceses huic S. Congregationi subjectae tamquam missiones haberi debeant."

regions which have an imperfect ecclesiastical structure, but also any territory which depends upon it, whether it is a question of an archdiocese, a diocese, a vicariate, a prefecture, or *missio sui iuris*.[29]

(2) The territories of the Latin Church which are under the jurisdiction of the Congregation for the Oriental Church can be considered as mission land, because, when the territories were transferred to the latter from the Congregation for the Propagation of the Faith in 1938,[30] the disciplinary status of the Latins involved was not changed. For instance, the terms vicariate, prefecture, etc., are used in the Latin territories depending upon the Congregation for the Oriental Church. If the Congregation for the Propagation of the Faith admits that there can be mission territories which are not under its competence, it is because they are considered to be such wherever the normal ecclesiastical hierarchy of the Latin rite is not yet constituted.

Paventi states that outside the territory depending upon the Congregation for the Propagation of the Faith, there can be no missions in a juridical sense, since other territories, such as those under the jurisdiction of the Consistorial Congregation and the Congregation for the Oriental Church, ought to be considered as outside the status of missions.[31] Moreover, he supports his opinion by quoting a conciliar decree of the first Council of China held in 1924: "Only one Congregation is competent to judge and to decide when and how a territory, having relinquished the status of mission and being removed from the jurisdiction of the Congregation for the Propagation of the Faith,

---

[29] S.C.P.F., decr. *Ad fluvium,* 4 maii 1910—*The Ecclesiastical Review,* XLIII (1910), 221-222. The first *missio sui iuris* was Drisdale River in Australia, founded in 1910. Cardinal Van Rossum used the term *missio sui iuris* for the first time to facilitate the entrance of new missionary groups in that mission. In 1931, there were 23 Latin missions of this kind. After the death of the Cardinal in 1932, the number decreased rapidly and in 1946 there were only six. At the present time, there are only two, according to the *Annuario Pontificio* for 1960, pp. 841-842. The term *missio sui iuris* is not found in the Code of Canon Law.

[30] Pius XI, motu propr. *Sancta Dei ecclesia,* 25 mart. 1938—*AAS* (1938), 157-158.

[31] Paventi, *Breviarium Iuris Missionalis,* p. 10, footnote n. 1.

can be subjected to and ruled by the common law.[32] Furthermore, he explains that this does not affect the fact that in the territories dependent upon the Congregation for the Oriental Church, mission works are performed to convert non-Catholics who still remain there. Missions of this kind cannot be considered foreign missions in the juridical sense, but only as home missions (Can. 1350, § 1).[33]

Paventi's opinion in this matter is not clear. The Congregation for the Oriental Church has jurisdiction over true mission territories, but only in the case of Latin territories subject to it. The "territory" of the Oriental rites outside the Oriental regions themselves may not be called mission territory at all, and the Congregation does not use the term.[34]

(3) Certain territories depending upon the Congregation for Extraordinary Ecclesiastical Affairs, e.g., the Portuguese Padroado, are also still considered as missions.[35]

Mission territory, then, may be defined as territory of the Latin rite where the ordinary hierarchy is not yet established, or if established, is still subject to the Congregation for the Propagation of the Faith, or remains in the status of mission under another Roman Congregation.

Many other territories have the character of missions *de facto*, but they are not considered as such, because they fall under the jurisdiction of the Consistorial Congregation.

> In reply to your letter, protocol 6008, dated the sixth of the current month, I make haste to answer you that there are no ecclesiastical districts of missionary character depending upon the Consistorial Congregation.[36]

[32] Paventi, *loc. cit.; Primum Concilium Sinense,* art. 58: "Unius Sedis Apostolicae est iudicare atque decernere quando et quomodo territorium aliquod, relicto statu missionis, ex iurisdictione S. Congregationis de Propaganda Fide iuri communi subiiciatur eoque regatur."

[33] Paventi, *loc. cit.*

[34] Pius XII, motu propr. *Postquam apostolicis litteris,* 9 febr. 1952, can. 303, § 1, nn. 2-3—*AAS,* XXXXIV (1952), 67-150.

[35] Paventi, *loc. cit.*

[36] Cf. *Annuario Missionario Italiano* (edite par l' U.M.C. d'Italie: Roma, 1942), p. 204, cited by Seumois, *Introduction a la Missiologie,* p. 74, foot-

B. *Teaching Office*

The final, fundamental charge of our Lord to His Apostles was that they should go forth and teach.[37]   The teaching office of the Church is that species of the jurisdictional power directed toward the propagation, preservation, and defense of the Catholic faith and exercised especially by the imposition of the precepts of faith within the competence of individual prelates.[38] The propagation of the faith, the preservation of the faith, and the defense of the faith are, therefore, the object of the teaching office.

To attain this triple objective effectively, the Church has at her command manifold means.   One of the efficacious means at the command of the Church is oral preaching, which is carried on by means of catechetical instruction, sermons, and missions.[39]

In general, preaching signifies the public manifestation of Christian doctrine with some authority, whether delegated or possessed by reason of an office.[40]   The term *praedicare* may be understood as something that is said before or in the presence of another, and it implies some kind of exhortation.[41]

Preaching of the Gospel and the teaching of Catholic doctrine are the most important objects of the Christian mission.   They are ordinarily described by such expressions as: *ad fidem in universo*

---

note n. 229: "In risposta alla lettera di V.S. Rev.ma, prot. 6008 del 6 corrente mese mi faccio premura significarle che non vi sono circoscrizioni ecclesiastiche di carattere missionario dipendenti dalla S.C. Consistoriale. Di V.S. Rev.ma, dev.mo B. Renzoni, Sost."

[37] Matthew 28:19. Cf. can. 1322; Leo XIII, ep. encycl. *Immortale Dei*, 1 nov. 1885—*AAS*, XVIII (1885), 174—*Fontes*, n. 592.

[38] Wernz-Vidal, *Ius Canonicum*, Vol. IV, n. 614; Coronata, *Institutiones Iuris Canonici*, Vol. II, n. 907; Pius XI, litt. encycl. *Ubi arcano Dei*, 23 dec. 1922—*AAS*, XIV (1922), 695; Ottaviani, *Institutiones Iuris Publici* (2 vols., Romae, 1935), Vol. II, n. 423; Pius XI, ep. *Dilecti filii*, 7 sept. 1923—*AAS*, XX (1928), 353.

[39] Can. 1327-1351.

[40] Coronata, *Institutiones Iuris Canonici*, Vol. II, n. 914.

[41] Allgeier, *The Canonical Obligation of Preaching in Parish Churches*, The Catholic University of America Canon Law Studies, n. 291 (Washington, D. C.: The Catholic University of America Press, 1949), p. 1.

mundo propagandam pertinentia cognoscant,[42] *opus adductionis animarum ad Ecclesiam Christi,*[43] *Christianae religionis catholicaeque fidei propagatio,*[44] *evangelicae veritatis lumen ubique diffundere,*[45] *Catholicam religionem propagare et stabilire,*[46] *Christianum nomen per universum orbem propagare,*[47] *qui laudabili zelo in pluribus missionibus ad fidei incrementum salutemque animarum adlaborant, etc.*[48]

The Congregation for the Propagation of the Faith has an official duty to extend, propagate, and spread the Gospel, that is, to evangelize, since the mission lands need and await the Gospel which is first of all a light that missionaries shine forth and a seed that they sow.[49]

The Gospel must be made known in all places and to all classes. Those who govern missions must keep striving to bring the Gospel to all parts of their territory.[50] Preaching the Gospel and teaching Catholic doctrine, thus, stand for the work of the missions as a whole.[51]

[42] Gregory XV, const. *Inscrutabili,* 22 iun. 1622—*Coll. S.C.P.F.,* I, n. 3.

[43] *Loc. cit.*

[44] Clement IX, const. *Sollicitudo,* 17 iun. 1669—*Coll. S.C.P.F.,* I, n. 181; Clement IX, const. *Speculatores,* 13 sept. 1669—*Coll. S.C.P.F.,* I, n. 186.

[45] Benedict XIV, const. *Ex quo singulari,* 5 iul. 1742—*Coll. S.C.P.F.,* I, n. 339.

[46] S.C.P.F., instr. *Neminem,* 23 nov. 1845—*Coll. S.C.P.F.,* I, n. 1002.

[47] S.C.P.F., ep. encycl. *Quamvis,* 20 oct. 1882—*Coll. S.C.P.F.,* II, n. 1577.

[48] S.C.P.F., ep. encycl. *Cum viris religiosis,* 30 iun. 1889—*Coll. S.C.P.F.,* II, n. 1606, ad VIII.

[49] *AAS,* XIII (1921), 562, 564; Pius XI, *homilia,* 4 iun. 1922—*AAS,* XIV (1922), 345; Pius X, allocutio, *Nostis,* 18 dec. 1924—*AAS,* XVI (1924), 490; Pius XI, litt. encycl. *Rerum ecclesiae,* 28 febr. 1926—*AAS,* XVIII (1926). 66; Pius XI, ep. *Ab ipsis,* 25 iun. 1926—*AAS,* XVIII (1926), 304-305; Pius XII, ep. encycl. *Saeculo exeunte,* 13 iun. 1940—*AAS,* XXXII (1940), 257, 259.

[50] Benedict XV, ep. ap. *Maximum illud,* 30 nov. 1919—*AAS,* XI (1919), 443; S.C.P.F., ep. *Sacrum consilium,* 16 apr. 1922—*AAS,* XIV (1922), 289; Pius XI, litt. encycl. *Rerum ecclesiae,* 28 febr. 1926—*AAS,* XVIII (1926), 79-81.

[51] *AAS,* XVIII (1926), 65. Cf. *AAS,* XI (1919), 445-446, 449.

C. *General Competence of the Congregation*

The Congregation for the Propagation of the Faith has the power to send and to recall the individuals needed for the missions, and has competence over whatever is connected with and necessary for the management of the missions.[52] Consequently, within the territories subject to it, the Congregation takes the place, in most matters, of the Consistorial Congregation,[53] the Congregation of the Sacraments (except for marriage cases),[54] the Congregation of the Council,[55] the Congregation of Sacred Rites (except for general norms governing the sacred liturgy and for beatification and canonization causes),[56] and the Congregation of Seminaries and Universities (except for the canonical erection and the supreme regulation of universities and seminaries of ecclesiastical studies.[57] By virtue of the decennial faculties received from the Roman Pontiff, the Congregation for the Propagation of the Faith can also grant these faculties to the local ordinaries of mission lands.[58]

The Congregation for the Propagation of the Faith, on the other hand, may not handle matters pertaining to the Holy Office (in cases concerning faith),[59] the Ceremonial Congregation,[60] the Congregation for Extraordinary Ecclesiastical Affairs,[61] the Congregation for the Oriental Church,[62] and the Sacred Penitentiary (in the internal forum).[63] Its jurisdiction is also limited by that

[52] Can. 252, § 1.

[53] Can. 248.

[54] Can. 249; 252, § 4.

[55] Can. 250.

[56] Can. 253.

[57] Can. 256; 252, § 3.

[58] *Periodica,* XLIX (1960), 341-352.

[59] Can. 247, §§ 3, 5; 252, § 4.

[60] Can. 254.

[61] Can. 255.

[62] Can. 257.

[63] Can. 258.

of the Congregation for Religious in matters concerning religious as such.[64]   By special privilege, however, some religious institutes are subject to the Congregation for the Propagation of the Faith even as regards internal discipline, contrary to the norm of Canon 252, § 5.[65]   With regard to the nature of the Congregation for the Propagation of the Faith, there are several points to be noted:

(1)   Nothing serious or of an extraordinary character may be decided by the Congregation, unless the Roman Pontiff has first been notified.[66]

(2)   All concessions and resolutions need papal approval, except those for which the Congregation has been given faculties to act.[67]

(3)   The Congregation for the Propagation of the Faith lacks judicial power, since the Code attributes judicial authority to tribunals.[68]

(4)   The Congregation may not interpret the Code authentically, since this is reserved to the Pontifical Commission for the Authentic Interpretation of the Code.[69]

(5)   The *motu proprio Cum iuris* of Benedict XV does not limit the power of the Congregation for the Propagation of the Faith to make particular laws or to interpret, restrict, and expand the laws it has already made for the missions.[70]

ARTICLE 3. CANON 252, § 2.

The first requirement for a synod in the missions is that it be an assembly of the clergy of a vicariate apostolic or an apostolic prefecture or a *missio sui iuris*.   In addition, the prescriptions of

[64] Can. 251; 252, § 5.

[65] Vromant, *De Personis*, p. 26.

[66] Can. 244, § 1.

[67] Can. 244, § 2.

[68] Can. 259.

[69] Benedict XV, motu propr. *Cum iuris*, 15 sept. 1917—*AAS*, IX (1917), 483-484.

[70] *Loc. cit.*

the common law concerning a diocesan synod are applicable, *congrua congruis referendo.* Thus it may be considered legitimate, so as to distinguish it from other clerical gatherings.

Convocation by the bishop is the second essential for the synod. He may exercise this act of jurisdiction himself or delegate another. But unless he is its author, the synod is convoked illegitimately.

The purpose of the synod constitutes the third element. This is stated in Canon 356, § 1. Since the bishop alone in his own territory has the power to make laws,[71] it is clear that he needs not convoke the synod to legislate for his territory. The purpose of the synod, therefore, can only be to enact laws after consulting the clergy about the needs of that territory.

Canon 304, § 2, prescribes that the regulations regarding plenary and provincial councils (can. 281-291) must be applied, *mutatis mutandis,* to the provinces or mission territories subject to the Congregation for the Propagation of the Faith. It is to be noted here that in mission territories where the ecclesiastical hierarchy is erected, the terms plenary and provincial are used for these councils. However, in those mission territories where the hierarchy is not erected, the terms general [72] regional council and regional [73] council may be employed for plenary and provincial councils respectively.

According to the Code of Canon Law, the Congregation for the Propagation of the Faith has an exclusive authority over all the decrees of the councils held in places subject to it and gives *recognition* to them.

> Curat ea omnia quae ad Conciliorum celebrationem et recognitionem in locis sibi subiectis pertinent.

A. *Nature of Synods*

The Congregation for the Propagation of the Faith has authority over everything related to the celebration and approval of councils and over meetings or conferences of bishops within

---

[71] Can. 362.

[72] Schmidlin, *Catholic Mission History,* p. 615.

[73] Grentrup, *Ius Missionarium,* pp. 40-41.

mission territories.[74]   Canon 252, § 2, concedes competence over the councils held in missionary districts to the Congregation, and does not mention synods, but it seems suitable to treat synods at this point.[75]   The reason that the Canon does not refer to synods is that statutes of the latter need not be submitted to the Holy See.

A synod is defined by Benedict XIV in his classical work, *De Synodo Dioecesana*, as a lawful assembly convoked by the bishop in which he gathers the priests and clerics of his diocese, and also all others who are bound to attend, for the purpose of deliberating and acting upon whatever concerns pastoral care.[76] By common law a diocesan synod must be held at least once every ten years.[77]   In regard to the obligation of celebrating a synod in both the abbey and prelature *nullius*, the Code has also imposed the obligation of celebrating the synod every ten years the same as every diocese.[78]   The only exception is if the territory has not at least three canonically established parishes.   In such a case the territory is governed by special law given by the Holy See, and therefore is not obligatory by the Code to celebrate the synod.[79]

Very often in the past the Congregation for the Propagation of the Faith commanded the vicar apostolic to hold synods very frequently in order to exchange advice and experience and to realize more clearly the measures that should be adopted for the benefit of the mission.[80]   The general principles of the common

[74] Can. 250, § 4.

[75] Can. 20.

[76] Benedict XIV, *De Synodo Dioecesana* (3 toms., Romae, 1783), Tom. I, lib. 1, cap. 1, n. 4; can. 356-358.

[77] Can. 356, § 1; *AAS*, XIII (1921), 291.

[78] Can. 215, § 2; 356, § 1.

[79] Can. 319, § 1.

[80] S.C.P.F., 12 iun. 1764—*Coll. S.C.P.F.*, I, n. 454—De Martinis, *Ius Pontificium*, I, Pars II, pp. 341-342: "EE. PP. decreverunt atque expresse mandarunt ut huiusmodi synodi sive congressus, ecclesiae disciplinae servandae apprime utiles, quam frequentissime potest . . ."; S.C.P.F., instr. *Neminem*, 23 nov. 1845—*Coll. S.S.*, n. 57: "Synodales saepe conventus celebrentur . . ."; S.C.P.F., instr. *Quando quidem*, 8 sept. 1869—*Coll. S.C.P.F.*, II, n.

law regarding diocesan synods are applicable, *congrua congruis referendo,* to the synod of an apostolic vicariate, with the exception that for the latter no time is determined. This determination is, thus, left to the prudent judgment of the vicar apostolic.[81] The phrase *congrua congruis referendo* means that the general norms relating to the celebration of synods should be transferred to the level of the mission, by adapting them to its conditions. Thus, it is that the provisions of the Code regarding presence at the synods of residential bishop, etc., will be applied equivalently to the synods of vicars apostolic.[82]

A synod held in an apostolic prefecture may be treated in the same way, although the Code is silent on the matter. According to the analogy of law, this conclusion may be drawn from Canon 304, § 2, which refers to apostolic prefectures, since § 1 of the same Canon (concerning the archives of the mission) places vicars and prefects apostolic on the same basis. Wernz-Vidal,[83] Toso,[84] Vito,[85] Vromant,[86] and Vermeersch,[87] with the exception of Chelodi [88] and Cappello [89] who deny to hold the synod, main-

---

1346; S.C.P.F., instr. *Quae a praesulis,* 18 oct. 1883—*Coll. S.C.P.F.,* II, n. 1606, V, ad 7, XIV; S.C.P.F., litt. encycl. *Inter ceteras,* 28 aug. 1893—*Coll. S.C.P.F.,* II, n. 1848; S.C.P.F., litt. encycl. 29 iul. 1889—*Coll. S.C.P.F.,* II, n. 2276.

[81] Can. 304, § 2; 356, § 1.

[82] Sartori, *Iuris Missionarii Elementa,* p. 28; Donnelly, *The Diocesan Synod,* The Catholic University of America Canon Law Studies, n. 74 (Washington, D. C.: The Catholic University of America, 1932), p. 43.

[83] *Ius de Personis* (Romae, 1928), II, 668.

[84] *Ad Codicem Iuris Canonici Benedicti XV Pontificis Maximi Auctoritate Promulgatum Commentaria Minora* (5 vols. in 2, Tiferni Tiberini, 1921-1927), III, 188 (hereafter referred to as *Commentaria Minora*).

[85] *Il Sinodo Diocesano* (Naples, 1928), pp. 21-22.

[86] *De Personis* (Louvain, Paris, Brussels, 1929), II, 174.

[87] *Periodica de Re Canonica et Morali,* IX (1921), 32; cf. Winslow, *Vicars and Prefects Apostolic,* The Catholic University of America Canon Law Studies, n. 24 (Washington, D. C.: The Catholic University of America, 1924), p. 51.

[88] *Summa Iuris Canonici* (3 vols., Romae, 1928), I, 356.

[89] *Ius de Personis iuxta Codicem Iuris Canonici* (2. ed., ab E. Bertagnolli

tain that a prefect apostolic while not being obliged to hold the synod can convoke one if he believes conditions warrant it. Apparently, this conclusion must be admitted as a consequence of Canon 294, § 1, which gives the prefect apostolic the powers of a residential bishop. There is no reason why the convocation of the synod can be excluded from this general concession.

The subject matter of synods should be particular things necessary or useful for the clergy and the people.[90] The vicar apostolic convokes the synod and presides over it. The vicar delegate may not do this, except with a special mandate, nor would a pro-vicar have this power *sede plena*.[91] The vicar apostolic is the sole legislator in the synod, others having only a consultative vote, and he alone signs the synodal decrees.[92]

Finally, it is clear from the words of Canon 8, § 1, "*Leges instituuntur cum promulgantur*," that synodal decrees must be promulgated before they have the force of law. An exact manner of promulgation has not been imposed by law, and therefore, according to Canon 335, § 2, the bishop or vicar apostolic is free to determine this. As soon as the statutes are promulgated, in whatever manner the bishop or vicar apostolic chooses, according to Canon 335, § 1 and 362, they oblige immediately, unless he expressly permits a period of *vacatio*, which is to be computed according to the norm of Canon 34, § 3, 2°.[93]

---

recognita et aucta Tridenti: Libr. Edit. Tridentinum, 1927), p. 398 (hereafter referred to as *Ius de Personis*).

[90] Can. 356, § 1; Benedict XIV, *De Synodo Dioecesana*, Tomus I, lib. IV, cap. V, ad V: "Itaque inter graviora negotia, in Dioecesana Synodo ab Episcopo tractanda et expedienda . . ."; *ibid.*, cap. VII.

[91] Can. 357, § 1; cf. can. 360-362.

[92] Can. 362.

[93] There is no need to submit the statutes of a synod to the Congregation for the Propagation of the Faith for review as is required by Canon 291 for the decrees of plenary and provincial councils. Cf. Benedict XIV, *De Synodo Dioecesana*, Tomus I, lib. XIII, cap. III, n. 6. However, if there is an unjust law included in the statutes, recourse may be had to the Congregation. Cf. Leo XIII, const. *Romanos pontifices*, 8 maii 1881, n. 13— *Fontes*, n. 582; Benedict XIV, *De Synodo Dioecesana*, Tomus I, lib. XIII, cap. V, n. 13.

B. *Nature and Recognition of Provincial or Regional Councils*

The Provincial Council is the legitimate assembly of the local ordinaries of an ecclesiastical province for the purpose of deliberating upon and providing for the ecclesiastical needs of that province.[94] In the territories subject to the Congregation for the Propagation of the Faith, provincial councils are held whereever there exists a territorial hierarchy according to the common law, consisting of canonically erected dioceses and provinces, for instance, in Japan, China, Australia, India, etc.[95]

According to the norms actually in force, what necessity is there to celebrate councils in the missions? The common law, prescribing the convocation of a provincial council in each ecclesiastical province at least once every twenty years, applies in general to the territories subject to the Congregation for the Congregation for the Propagation of the Faith where the ordinary hierarchy is established. Nevertheless, no fixed time is provided for the celebration of these councils in such territories.[96]

The provincial councils combine effectively the benefits of local legislation and of central authority in an eminently practical way. That unity, which is the chief mark of the Church, becomes most strikingly apparent to those outside the fold whenever there is uniformity, so far as possible, in matters of discipline, and this is a specific end of provincial legislation.[97]

In regard to recognition, Canon 291, § 1, states that before promulgation conciliar decrees are to be sent for examination to the Congregation of the Council.[98] The Congregation for the

[94] Wernz-Vidal, *Ius Canonicum*, II, 670, 681; Beste, *Instructio in Codicem* (2. ed., Collegeville, Minn.: St. John's Abbey Press, 1944), p. 231; Chelodi, *Ius de Personis*, p. 386.

[95] Sartori, *Iuris Missionarii Elementa*, p. 28.

[96] Can. 283; 304, § 2.

[97] S.C.P.F., litt. encycl. *Inter ceteras*, 28 aug. 1893—*Coll. S.C.P.F.*, II, n. 1848; Murphy, *Legislative Powers of the Provincial Council*, The Catholic University of America Canon Law Studies, n. 257 (Washington, D. C.: The Catholic University of America Press, 1947), p. 28.

[98] Coronata (*Institutiones*, I, 424, footnote n. 7) explains that the statutes are examined by one consultor, then by all the consultors (or at least five of them), and finally by all the Cardinals of the Congregation.

Propagation of the Faith is competent to examine and inspect the acts and decrees of councils held in mission territories, just as the Congregation of the council is competent for those territories which are subject to the Consistorial Congregation.[99]

The decrees in question do not have the force of law, until they are reviewed by the Congregation for the Propagation of the Faith and are subsequently promulgated.[100] Without the antecedent *recognitio* of the latter the promulgation of the decrees of councils held in mission territories would be not only illicit, but also invalid.[101] The conclusive argument for the invalidity of conciliar decrees not so reviewed or examined arises from the fact that this forms part of the constitutive common law affecting the provincial council,[102] and consequently must be interpreted according to the norms of the former law,[103] since Canon 291, § 1, does not express any change in the matter.[104] *Recognitio* was known by pre-Code authors as an indispensable element of conciliar law and as a *conditio sine qua non* for the force of that law.[105] Post-Code authors have retained this position of

[99] S.C. Consist., *Dubia de competentia,* 12 nov. 1908, ad VII—*AAS,* I (1909), 150, 152: "Utrum acta Conciliorum, quae celebrari contigerint in territorio Congregationi de Propaganda relicto, remittenda sint ad Congregationem Concilii. Ad VII Negative." Cf. can. 250, § 4; 252, § 2; 304, § 2.

[100] Can. 8, § 1; Michiels, *Normae Generales,* I, 149, 151; Van Hove, *De Legibus,* pp. 112, 115.

[101] Wernz-Vidal, *Ius Canonicum,* II, 683; Coronata, *Institutiones,* I, 424, footnote n. 8.

[102] Wernz-Vidal, *op. cit.,* II, 673.

[103] "Provincialium vero, ubivis terrarum illae celebrentur, decreta ad se [S.C.C.] mitti praecipiet, eaque singula expendet et recognoscet." Sixtus V, bull, *Immensa aeterni,* 22 ian. 1588—*Bull. Rom.,* VIII, 991. Cf. Wernz, *Ius Decretalium,* Vol. I, n. 181, footnote n. 42: "Ante recognitionem illam factam acta et decreta Concil. partic. promulgari valide non possunt." Cf. S.C.C., 6 apr. 1596. This declaration cannot be found in Fontes or the *Coll. S.C.P.F.,* but it is quoted by Petra (*Commentaria ad Constitutiones Apostolicas* [5 vols. in 2, Venetiis, 1729], I, 284, n. 121): "Decreta, quae in Conciliis Provincialibus conduntur, publicari non debent inconsulto Romano Pontifice."

[104] Cf. can. 6, n. 2.

[105] Petra, *Commentaria ad Constitutiones Apostolicas* (5 vols. in 2, Venetiis, 1729), I, 284, n. 121: "Et omnes docent, ut transmittantur statuta

the absolute necessity of *recognitio* for the validity of the conciliar decrees.[106]

C. *Nature and Recognition of Plenary (National) or General Regional Councils*

The Plenary Council is the legitimate assembly of the ordinaries of several ecclesiastical provinces under the presidency of a delegate of the Holy See for the purpose of deliberating upon and making decrees for ecclesiastical needs.[107]   Plenary councils according to Canon 281 may be celebrated even in mission territories, but there is no obligation to do so.[108]

As indicated in Canon 281, a plenary council requires for its celebration the permission of the Roman Pontiff, and it also presupposes that the Roman Pontiff's legate convokes the council and presides over it.   A legitimate convocation, therefore, is needed, because otherwise it would be wanting in judicial authority.[109]   The territories which are governed by the conciliar decrees of a plenary council are usually, but not necessarily, coterminous with a nation.   When in fact a plenary council is attended by the ordinaries of all the ecclesiastical provinces of a nation, it is called a national council.[110]   Thus, any council which

---

haec Conciliaria Papae, qui solet ea approbare, medio oraculo Sac. Congre. Concilii, nec possunt imprimi, aut executioni demandari sine dicta facultate . . . ac est dispositum in Constitutione Sixti V." Cf. Fagnanus, *Commentaria in Quinque Decretalium Libros*, lib. V, tit. I, cap. 25, n. 95; Gousset, *Exposition des Principes du Droit Canonique*, p. 296; Bouix, *De Concilio Provinciali* (3. ed., Parisiis, 1884), p. 371; Scherer, *Handbuch des Kirchenrechtes* (2 vols., Graz-Leipzig, 1886-1898), I, 674.

[106] Cf. *supra*, p. 72.

[107] Wernz, *Ius Decretalium*, Vol. II, n. 843.

[108] Can. 304, § 2; Sartori, *Iuris Missionarii Elementa*, p. 29; Grentrup, *Ius Missionarium*, p. 41.

[109] Can. 304; 281; Toso, *Commentaria Minora*, III, 104.   There is an exception concerning the Papal Legate in the countries, which have concordats with the Holy See, for instance, in Portugal the Archbishop of Goa has the right to preside at the plenary council for all the territories of East-Indies. Cf. De Martinis, *Ius Pontificium*, VII, appendix XXI, art. II, 349; Grentrup, *op. cit.*, p. 42.

[110] Wernz-Vidal, *Ius Canonicum*, II, 676; Vermeersch, *Epitome*, Vol. I, n. 394.

embraces more than one ecclesiastical province and is at the same time less than an ecumenical council of the Church is a plenary council.[111]

In the territories subject to the Congregation for the Propagation of the Faith, where a canonically erected hierarchy according to the common law does not exist, the rules of the Code on plenary and provincial councils (canons 281-291) extend to the general regional or regional councils, insofar as these norms are applicable.[112] If a regional council is held with the permission of the Roman Pontiff and under the presidency of the papal legate, it may assimilated to a plenary council. This was the case with the council celebrated in Shanghai, China, in 1924, in Indochina, in 1934, and in Australia and New-Zealand, in 1937.[113] In other cases, if a regional council is held without the permission of the Roman Pontiff and without the presidency of the papal legate, it is, then, assimilable to a provincial council and does not have the character of a plenary council. Consequently, it is called quasi-provincial or simply regional. A decree of June 23, 1879, divided China into five distinct areas and prescribed the holding of regional councils in each of them.[114] Later, new districts for holding regional councils were simply established outside China.[115]

The question arises whether the time and place for the celebration of a plenary council is or is not determined by law. When the nature of the plenary council is considered, it appears that the designation of time and place is not a matter to be specifically determined by law. Canon 281 simply states that a plenary council cannot be celebrated without the permission

[111] Toso, *Commentaria Minora*, III, 103.

[112] Can. 304, § 2.

[113] Pius X, litt. *Quamquam*, 20 ian. 1924—*AAS*, XVI (1924), 92; *Primum Concilium Sinense—Acta—Decreta et Normae*, etc. (Zi-Ka-Wei, 1924), pp. 5-6; Sartori, *op. cit.*, p. 29; Grentrup, *op. cit.*, pp. 41-42.

[114] S.C.P.F., decr. *Vicarium divisionem*, 23 iun. 1879—*Coll. S.C.P.F.*, II, n. 1524.

[115] S.C.P.F., litt. 17 apr. 1884—*Analecta Iuris Pontificii*, XXIII (1884), 1021-1023. Cf. Grentrup, *op. cit.*, pp. 40-41.

of the Roman Pontiff,[116] i.e., the Holy Father must approve the time and the place selected, or designate another time and place in lieu of the former.

As regards the manner of celebrating a plenary council in mission territories, the rules of the common law are applicable, *congrua congruis referendo.*[117] In regard to *recognitio,* the conciliar decrees should be sent to the Congregation for the Propagation of the Faith for examination. This has to be done before their promulgation.[118] After the censorship or correction made by the Congregation, the decrees must be promulgated in order to have juridic efficacy.[119] In addition, it may be noted that censorship or correction made by the Congregation does not give the decrees a pontifical authority, nor do they receive thereby any positive ratification; it is merely a condition of their legitimate promulgation and validity.[120] From what has been said, it can be understood that there is a clear distinction between papal laws and those of a plenary council. This is not merely a speculative distinction, since Canon 82 gives different principles on dispensation from these laws.[121]

[116] "Ordinarii plurium provinciarum ecclesiasticum in Concilium plenarium convenire possunt, petita tamen venia a Romano Pontifice. . . . "

[117] Can. 281-291.

[118] Can. 291, § 1; Olarte, *The Plenary Council,* The Catholic University of America Canon Law Studies, n. 372 (Washington, D. C.: The Catholic University of America Press, 1958), pp. 94-95.

[119] Can. 8, § 1; Michiels, *Normae Generales,* I, 185.

[120] S.C.C., 19 febr. 1921—*AAS,* XIII (1921), 228: "Namque approbatio S. Sedis, quae mere conditio est legitima promulgationis nullam positivam S. Sedis auctoritatem ad ista decreta superaddit." Cf. Chelodi, *Ius de Personis,* p. 393.

[121] Can. 82—Bishops and other local ordinaries can dispense from diocesan laws, from the laws of provincial and plenary councils, according to the rule of Canon 291, § 2, but they cannot dispense from laws which the Roman Pontiff has especially decreed for a particular territory, except in the case indicated in Canon 81.

CHAPTER V

LIMITATION OF THE PRESENT COMPETENCE OF THE CONGREGATION

ARTICLE 1. CANON 252, § 3.

On the basis of the territory of the missions involved, the constitution *Sapienti consilio* imposed a new restriction upon the Congregation for the Propagation of the Faith.[1] In turn, the Code incorporated the restriction of the constitution *Sapienti consilio* into the text of the law.[2] Now the territorial jurisdiction of this Congregation is limited *de jure* almost exclusively to the missions among pagans or infidels in lands of the Latin Church which are subject to it.[3]

The Code of Canon Law attributes to the Congregation for the Propagation of the Faith not only the mission territories proper, but also a certain number of areas where the ordinary hierarchical structure remains somewhat incomplete.[4] The field of the Congregation suffered a substantial reduction in 1908,[5] when the constitution *Sapienti consilio* withdrew certain countries from its authority, and transferred them to the rule of the common law.

On the other hand, some mission territories which, for political reasons, had previously depended upon the Congregation for Extraordinary Ecclesiastical Affairs, were subjected to the Congregation for the Propagation of the Faith.[6]

---

[1] Pius X, const. *Sapienti consilio*, 22 iun. 1908—*AAS*, I (1909), n. 6.

[2] Can. 252, § 3.

[3] *Guida*, p. 39.

[4] Cf. can. 252, § 3.

[5] Pius X, const. *Sapienti consilio*, 22 iun. 1908—*AAS*, I (1909), 12-13.

[6] S.C. Consist., *Dubia de competentia*, I, 12 nov. 1908—*AAS*, I (1909), p. 148.

Finally, by the *motu proprio Sancta Dei ecclesia* of Pius XI, many countries were transferred from the control of the Congregation for the Propagation of the Faith to the Congregation for the Oriental Church.[7]

The last part of Canon 252, § 3, states that societies of ecclesiastics and seminaries, exclusively intended for the training of foreign missioners are to be subject to the Congregation for the Propagation of the Faith.

> Eius iurisdictio iis est circumscripta regionibus, ubi, sacra hierarchia nondum constituta, status missionis perseverat. Huic Congregationi sunt etiam subiectae regiones, quae etsi hierarchia inibi constituta sit, adhuc inchoatum aliquid praeseferunt. Eidem pariter subsunt societates ecclesiasticorum ac Seminaria quae exclusive fundata sunt eo fine, ut in eis instituantur missionarii pro exteris missionibus, praesertim quod attinet ad eorum regulas, administrationem atque opportunas concessiones ad sacram ordinationem alumnorum requisitas.

A. *Limitation of the Actual Mission Territories Depending upon the Congregation*

The first part of Canon 252, § 3, distinguishes missions into two classes. Missions of the first class are (1) archdioceses, and (2) dioceses; missions of the second class (called quasi-dioceses) are (1) vicariates apostolic, (2) prefectures apostolic, (3) *missiones sui iuris.* An *abbatia* or *praelatura nullius*, which may be considered as a diocese, may pertain to the first class.[8] Those countries in which no ecclesiastical hierarchy (archdioceses, dioceses) has been erected, but where rather the mission organization (vicariates, prefectures) still prevails, are considered the mission territories governed by the supreme authority of the Church. Consequently, the missions comprise basically only those territories in which no hierarchy of residential bishops has been erected. As a basic differentiating mark between missions

---

[7] Pius XI, motu propr. *Sancta Dei ecclesia*, 25 mart. 1938—*AAS*, XXX (1938), 157-159.

[8] Can. 215, § 2: "In iure nomine dioecesis venit quoque abbatia vel praelatura nullius." Cf. Paventi, *Breviarium Iuris Missionalis*, p. 11. For further divisions of the missions, this work may be consulted, *loc. cit.*

and other ecclesiastical territories, the latter falling under the jurisdiction of the Consistorial Congregation, the external constitutional form, i.e., the existence or non-existence of the hierarchical organization, has first to be considered.[9] This principle, however, is incomplete. Many territories still remain subject to the Congregation for the Propagation of the faith, in which the ecclesiastical hierarchy has already been established for a shorter or a longer period but, which remain nevertheless in a precarious and provisional condition, still in the initial stage of hierarchical organization and hence not yet divested completely of the character of mission territories.[10]

These conditions, which may be due to material deficiences, a lack of resources, and, above all, lack of native clergy, offer a factual basis to determine which territories belong to the missions. According to Canon 252, § 3, moreover, all the territories subject to the Congregation for the Propagation of the Faith may be so considered. It seems clear that the lack of native clergy is the most critical factor, because the other two conditions are fulfilled when the people furnish clerics to the Church for major as well as for minor functions. This is entirely a question of a native clergy.

In 1919 Benedict XV issued the apostolic letter *Maximum illud*, in which he emphasized the necessity of a native clergy:

> Wherever there exists a native clergy adequate in numbers, well trained, and worthy of its holy vocation, there you can rightly say that the work of the missionaries is successfully finished and that the Church is well founded.[11]

In 1923 the Congregation for the Propagation of the Faith sent a letter to all missionary religious institutes in which it stated:

[9] Hilling, "Die rechtliche Stellung der Propagandakongregation nach der neuen Kurialreform Pius X," *Zeitschrift für Missionwissenschaft*, I (1911), 148.

[10] Hilling, *loc. cit.*

[11] Benedict XV, ep. ap. *Maximum illud*, 30 nov. 1919—*AAS*, XI (1919), 445: "Ubicumque igitur adsit quantum sat est indigenae cleri eiusque bene institui et vocatione sua sancta digni, ibi Missionarii opus feliciter expletum ecclesiamque praeclare esse fundatam iure dixeris."

It is of the greatest importance that superiors pay attention to the formation of native clergy in the missions entrusted to their institutes. And indeed this is necessary, because the various territories were committed to them precisely for the purpose of founding and establishing the Church there.[12]

In 1926 Pius XI mentioned in the encyclical letter *Rerum ecclesiae* that native priests must be trained to govern the Church in their own lands, according to the practice begun by the Apostles themselves.

And how shall the Church hold together firmly in pagan lands today, unless it is composed of all those elements from which it once developed among us, that is, from the people and clergy of each region, and from their own men and women religious? [13]

In the same passage, Pius XI commanded the formation of native clergy:

And first of all we call your attention to the great importance of forming a native clergy. You should do this with all energy. Otherwise we maintain that your apostolate will be lacking something, and still more that it will be too long impeded and delayed in setting up and organizing the Church in those regions.[14]

In addition, the Pope insisted on the need for native vocations to religious institutes: "One of the principal duties of the head of missions is to erect native religious communities of men and of women." [15]

In the same year, 1926, Pius XI sent a special letter to China,

[12] S.C.P.F., decr. *Cum prefectura apostolica*, 20 mart. 1923—*AAS*, XV (1923), 370.

[13] Pius XI, litt. encycl. *Rerum ecclesiae*, 18 febr. 1926—*AAS*, XVIII (1926), 74: "Et unde haec apud ethnicos hodie constabit, nisi ex omnibus iis elementis, ex quibus apud nos olim coaluit, id est ex suo cuiusque regionis et populo et clero suisque religiosis viris ac feminis?"

[14] *AAS*, XVIII (1926), 73: "Ac primum omnium, cogitationes eo vestras revocamus, quanti intersit, indigenas in clerum cooptari: quod nisi pro viribus effeceritis, non tam mancum fore censemus apostolatum vestrum; quam Ecclesiae in regionibus istis constitutioni atque ordinationi diutius moram allatum iri ac tarditatem."

[15] *Ibid.*, p. 77.

in which he opposed the false ideas of foreign missionaries in that country and directed that they should receive promising native boys for proper training and ultimately for ordination to the priesthood, "since it has been its [the Holy See's] conviction that in no other way can Christ's kingdom be set up and established anywhere." [16]

In 1944 at the assembly of the directors and officials of the pontifical mission organization in Rome, Pius XII delivered an allocution in which he said:

> The great purpose of the missions is to establish the Church in the new lands and to make it take solid roots there, in such a way that it can one day live and develop itself without the support of the work of the missions. The work of the missions is not the end in itself; it tends earnestly toward that other higher end, but retires once that has been attained.[17]

From these citations the following observation can be made. The work of the missionary is completed and the Church is founded when it depends on itself alone, and the work of the missions retires when this purpose has been attained. Moreover, a norm is set down for determining when the work of the missions is finished. Only, then, can an ordinary hierarchical Church be considered established in a region when it functions by itself, with its own churches, with its own local native clergy, with its own means, in a word, when it depends only upon itself.[18]

---

[16] Pius XI, ep. *Ab ipsis,* 15 iun. 1926—*AAS,* XVIII (1926), 305: "Ut puerulos indigenas bonae spei rite instituendos et aliquando sacerdotio initiandos susciperent, cum sibi persuasum esset, haud aliter Christi regnum ubivis constitui ac stabiliri posse."

[17] Pius XII, allocution, *Vivamento gradito,* 24 iun. 1944—*AAS,* XXXVI (1940), 210: "Il grande scopo delle Missioni è di stabilire la Chiesa nelle nuove terre e di farle ivi mettere salde radici tanto da poter un giorno vivere e svilupparsi senza il sostegno dell'Opera delle Missioni. L'Opera delle missioni non è scopo a se medesima: essa tende con ardore a quell' alto fine, ma si ritira quando è stato raggiunto."

[18] S.C.P.F., decr. *Lo sviluppo,* 20 mart. 1923—*AAS,* XV (1923), 370, III; *Sylloge,* n. 112: "Solo allora può dirsi fondata la Chiesa in una regione, quando essa ivi si regga de sè, con proprie chiese, con proprio clero nativo del luogo, con propri mezzi; in una parola, quando essa non dipenda ivi

B. *Geographical Distribution of the Missions Subject to the Congregation*

First of all, the Congregation for the Propagation of the Faith reserves the term *missio sui iuris* in a special way as a step in territorial organization inferior to or prior to the apostolic prefecture. This juridical form does not appear in the Code of Canon Law. It falls under the Congregation and is even, one could say, characteristic of the labors of Cardinal Van Rossum.[19]

Apart from this, the first step in the canonical organization of the missions is usually a territory headed by a prelate with the title of prefect apostolic. He is usually not a bishop, but one who has a vicarious ordinary jurisdiction over a mission territory.[20] The second step is the establishment of a vicariate apostolic, where regularly a titular bishop has a vicarious ordinary jurisdiction. In the words of the Code, vicars and prefects apostolic are those who rule mission territories which are not yet erected into dioceses.[21]

In addition, mention may be made of other exceptional territorial divisions found in the missions. The *abbatia* or *praelatura nullius* is an exempt territory to the complete exclusion of the jurisdiction of the bishop. This territory has been actually separated from an existing diocese in such a way that it is no longer a part of that diocese.[22]

When the vicariates apostolic of a given area are relatively self-sufficient and when local conditions make permanent status desirable, the vicariates are raised to diocesan or archdiocesan rank.[23] In view of these several classes of mission territories

---

che da se stessa." *Primum Concilium Sinense*, n. 8: "Tunc solum Ecclesia in aliqua regione fundata potest dici, quando ipsa sibi sufficit, propriis ecclesiasticis aedificiis, proprio indigena clero, propriisque opibus suffulta."

[19] Seumois, *Introduction a la Missiologie*, p. 78, footnote n. 241.

[20] Linskey, *op. cit.*, p. 50; can. 293, § 1.

[21] Can. 293, § 1.

[22] Benko, *The Abbot Nullius*, The Catholic University of America Canon Law Studies, n. 173 (Washington, D. C.: The Catholic University of America Press, 1943), p. 10.

[23] M. Martin, *op. cit.*, p. 64; Linskey, *op. cit.*, p. 51.

subject to the Congregation for the Propagation of the Faith, it may be useful to enumerate below all the territories which are under the jurisdiction of the Congregation.[24]   The territories which are not followed by a parenthesis in the following list depend *in toto* on the Congregation for the Propagation of the Faith. Those which are followed by a parenthesis are not dependent on this Congregation except in part, as indicated within the parentheses.   In the list, these abbreviations are used:

AD. : Archdiocese
D. : Diocese
AN. : *Abbatia nullius*
VA. : Vicariate Apostolic
PA. : Prefecture Apostolic

I. ASIA

Japan, Korea, China, Hongkong, Philippine Islands (VA. Calapan, Jolo, Mountin Province, Palawan), Vietnam, Laos, Cambodia, Thailand, Burma, South India (except those territories which depend upon the Congregation for the Oriental Church), East Pakistan, Ceylon, North India, West Pakistan, Arabia, Kuwait, Malaya Federation, Indonesia including Borneo, Celebes, Java, Lesser Sunda Islands, Moluccas, Sumatra, Sulawesi, Timor, Flores.

II. AFRICA

1. NORTH AND NORTHEAST: Algeria (D. Laghoust), South Ethiopia (VA. Gimma, Harar; PA. Hosanna, Neghelli), Somalia, Libia, Morocco, French Somalia (D. Djibouti), Sudan.

2. EAST: Kenya and Zanzibar, Nyasaland, North Rhodesia, Tanganyika, Uganda.

3. WEST: French West Africa, including Dahomey, French Guinea, French Soudan, Ivory Coast, Niger, Senegal, including Mauritania, Upper Volta, British Cameroons, Costa d'Oro, Portuguese Guinea, British Gambia, Liberia, Nigeria, Sierra Leone, French Togo, Ghana.

---

[24] Cf. *Atlas Missionum a Sacra Congregatione de Propaganda Fide Dependentium* cura editus eiusdem Sacrae Congregationis studio autem P. Henrici Emmerich (Vatican City, 1958), pp. 1-44.

4. CENTRAL: French Equatorial Africa, French Cameroon, Belgian Congo, Spanish Guinea.

5. SOUTH: Basutoland, South Rhodesia, Swaziland, Union of South Africa.

6. AFRICAN ISLANDS: Madagascar, Reunion Island, Mauritius Islands, Seychelles Islands.

III. EUROPE

North Albania (AD. Durres; D. Pult, Sape, Lezho; AN. Orosh), Yugoslavia (AD. Bar, Vinbosno; D. Banjaluka, Mostar, Skoplje), Denmark, Norway, Sweden, Finland, Gibraltar, Iceland.

IV. AMERICA

1. NORTH: Alaska, Canada (VA. Grouard, Hudson Bay, James Bay, Keewatin, Labrador, Mackenzie, Prince Rupert, Whitehorse), Bermuda (VA. Bermuda Islands).

2. CENTRAL: French Guiana, Dutch Guiana, British Guiana, Venezuela (VA. Caroni, Machiques, Puerto Ayacucho, Ticupita), Colombia (VA. Barranca, Bermeja, Buenaventura, Casanare, Florentia, Istinina, Riohacha, Quibdo, San Jorge, Sibundoy, Vallendupar, Villavicencio; PA. Arauca, Guapi, Leticia, Mitu, San Andres y Providencia, Tierradentro, Tumaco, Vichada), British Caribbean Federation including Trinidad, Grenada, St. Louis, Dominica, French Antilles, Curaçao, Jamaica, Bahama, Panama (VA. Darien), Costa Rica (VA. Limon), Nicaragua (VA. Bluefield), Honduras (VA. San Petro Sula), British Honduras (D. Belize), Mexico (VA. Tarahumaro, Tijuana; PA. La Paz).

3. SOUTH: Paraguay (VA. Charco Paraguayo), Bolivia (VA. Chiquitos, Cuevo, Beni, Reyes, Rufio de Chavez, Pando), Ecuador (VA. Esmeraldes, Mendez, Napo; PA. Aguarico, Canelos, San Miguel de Succumbios, Zamera), Peru (VA. Iquitos, Pucallpa, Puerto Maldonado, Requena, San Gabriel de Maranon, San Jose de Amazonas, San Ramon; PA. San Francisco Javier), Chile (VA. Araucania, Aysen).

V. OCEANIA

Marquenzas Islands, Tahiti Islands, Cook Islands, Tonga Islands, Samoa Tokelau Islands, Wallis Islands, Fiji Islands, Gilbert Islands, New Hebrides Islands, New Ireland, New Britain, Nouvelle Caledonie, Guam, Marianna Islands, Marshall Islands, Western Solomon Islands, New Guinea, New Zealand, Australia.

C. *Ecclesiastical Societies and Seminaries Destined Exclusively for the Foreign Missions*

The foreign mission can be defined as the part of the ecclesiastical ministry directed toward the preparation and consolidation of the true faith among pagans or dissident Christians. The legitimate authority of the foreign mission comes from the mandate of the Church, without which there is no genuine mission. The activity of this mission begins with the preaching of the Gospel and proceeds until full pastoral functions are achieved, i.e., the administration of the sacraments and sacramentals, the giving of instructions, etc. These pastoral functions include, besides the divine worship, whatever serves the purposes of missions, e.g., hospitals, schools, hotels, orphanages, printing facilities, asylums for lepers, organizations for workers and farmers, etc.[25]

This definition expresses the primary concept of missions, which is to lay the foundation for the establishment of the faith and to increase the number of the faithful. The foreign missions are directed toward pagans, or toward all the non-baptized in general, such as Mohammedans and Jews. But what of heretics and schismatics? It is the common opinion among Catholic authors (except Schmidlin, Streit, etc.), that the object of the foreign missions is also applicable to heretics and schismatics. There are many pontifical documents to this effect.[26]

---

[25] Sartori, *op. cit.*, p. 12; Benedict XV, ep. ap. *Maximum illud,* 30 nov. 1919—*AAS,* XI (1919), 444; S.C.P.F., ep. *Sacrum consilio,* 16 apr. 1922—*AAS,* XIV (1922), 296.

[26] S.C.P.F., const. *Inscrutabili,* 22 iun. 1622—*Coll. S.C.P.F.,* I, n. 3; Leo XII, encycl. *Sancta Dei civitas,* 3 dec. 1880—*Coll. S.C.P.F.,* II, n. 1543; Urban VIII, const. *Immortalis Dei,* 1 aug. 1627—De Martinis, *Ius Pontificium,* I, 1; S.C.P.F., encycl. *Ad omnes,* 15 ian. 1622—*Collectio Lacensis—Acta et Decreta Sacrorum Conciliorum Recentiorum* (7 vols., Friburgi-Brisgoviae, 1870-1890), VII, 683. "Codex rem non definivit; at in can. 1350, § 2 favet huic sententiae, adhibendo verbum acatholicos, quod desig-

Canons 673-681 deal with the societies of men and women living in common without vows. When they are clerical societies and are engaged exclusively in the work of the foreign missions, they are *de iure* subject to the Congregation for the Propagation of the Faith.[27] Those clerical societies which are not engaged exclusively in the work of the foreign missions, even though some of their members are so engaged, are ordinarily subject to the Congregation for Religious.[28] Moreover, clerical societies which are limited to a nation with which the Holy See has a concordat may be subject to the Congregation for Extraordinary Ecclesiastical Affairs.[29]

In 1909 and 1910, the Consistorial Congregation, then commissioned to decide the questions of competence among the Roman dicasteries, declared that missionary institutes were subject to the Congregation for the Propagation of the Faith.[30] The Code of Canon Law has incorporated this decision. Even if such institutes have their principal house in a diocese not subject to the Congregation for the Propagation of the Faith, they fall under the jurisdiction of this Congregation.

The fourteen missionary societies and seminaries of pontifical approval, especially and exclusively destined for the foreign missions, under the authority of the Congregation for the Propagation of the Faith, are: [31]

---

nat tam baptizatos quam non baptizatos." Sartoii, *Iuris Missionarii Elementa,* p. 11, n. 6.

[27] Can. 252, § 3.

[28] Can. 255.

[29] Can. 251, § 1.

[30] S.C. Consist., Romana, *In generali conventu,* 10 dec. 1909—*AAS,* I (1909), 815; S.C. Consist., Romana, *Quaesitum,* 15 mart. 1910—*AAS,* II (1910), 230.

[31] *Annuario Pontificio* for 1960, pp. 899-904; Heimbucher, *Die Orden und Kongregationen der katholischen Kirche* (3. ed., 2 vols., Paderborn, 1933-1934), II, 600-610; Stanton, *De Societatibus sive Virorum sive Mulierum in Communi Viventium sine Votis* (Halifaxiae, 1936), pp. 41-44, 77-82, 88, 121; Paventi, *De Iuramento ac de Titulo Missionis* (Romae, 1943), p. 87; Paventi, *Organización del Instituto Español del S. Francisco Javier para Missiones Extranjeras Commentario y Exposición de las Constitutiones* (Burgos: Aldecoa, 1950), p. 60; Nugent, *Ordination in Societies of the Common Life,*

1. Paris Foreign Mission Society (founded in Paris, 1660; approved August 11, 1664.
2. White Fathers (founded in Algeria, 1868; received the decree of praise March 16, 1879; approved February 15, 1908).
3. Society of Missionaries to Africa (founded in Lyons, 1856; received the decree of praise November 1, 1890; approved August 23, 1900).
4. Society of Missionaries of Saint Joseph of Mill Hill (founded in England, 1866; received the decree of praise January 28, 1897; approved in 1908).
5. Society of Maryknoll for Foreign Missions (founded in New York, 1911; received the decree of praise July 23, 1915; approved in 1930).
6. Society of Saint Columbans for the Missions in China (founded in Ireland, 1917; approved June 5, 1925).
7. Pontifical Institute of the Holy Apostles Peter and Paul and of Saints Ambrose and Charles for the Foreign Missions (The Foreign Mission Institute of Milan had been founded in 1850. The Pontifical Seminary of Saints Peter and Paul in Rome was founded in 1874. Pius XI united the Foreign Mission Institute of Milan with the Pontifical Seminary of Saints Peter and Paul in Rome May 23, 1926).
8. Foreign Mission Society of the Province of Québec (founded in Montreal, 1921; approved July 15, 1929).
9. Foreign Mission Society of Bethlehem in Switzerland (founded in Switzerland, 1921; approved March 4, 1936).
10. Scarboro Foreign Mission Society (founded in Canada, 1918; approved June 11, 1940).
11. Spanish Institute of Saint Francis Xavier for the Foreign Missions (founded in Spain, 1899; approved June 18, 1947).
12. Yarumal Institute for the Foreign Missions (founded in Colombia, 1939; approved January 16, 1953).

The Catholic University of America Canon Law Studies n. 341 (Washington, D. C.: The Catholic University of America Press, 1958), pp. 1-13.

13. Mexican Seminary for the Foreign Missions (founded in Mexico, 1949; approved April 28, 1953).
14. Society of Saint Patrick for the Foreign Missions (founded in Ireland, 1932; received the decree of praise December 9, 1958).

With regard to seminaries, the constitution *Deus scientiarum Dominus* deals with certain types of seminaries and universities, and not with all institutions of this kind. Seminaries in mission countries as well as seminaries pursuing exclusively mission purposes are subject to the Congregation for the Propagation of the Faith.[32]

> The canonical erection and supreme direction of any university or faculty of ecclesiastical studies, even in places or in institutes subject to the Congregation for the Oriental Church or the Congregation for the Propagation of the Faith, and even of faculties for any groups of families of religious, is reserved to the Sacred Congregation of Seminaries and Universities.[33]

It is to be noted that the reference is to pontifical faculties and universities. Hence ordinary seminaries in mission territories are not affected by this constitution and remain subject to the Congregation for the Propagation of the Faith.[34]

The Congregation for the Propagation of the Faith possesses jurisdiction *de facto* not only over the societies and seminaries mentioned in Canon 252, § 3, but also over the various congregations and religious colleges of which it authorizes the foundation,

[32] Pius X, const. *Deus scientiarum Dominus*, 24 maii 1931, art. 4—*AAS*, XXIII (1931), 243-262.

[33] *Loc. cit.:* "Canonica erectio et suprema moderatio cuiusvis Universitatis et Facultatis studiorum ecclesiasticorum, in locis quoque et Institutis quae Sacris Congregationis pro Ecclesia Orientali et de Propaganda Fide subiecta sunt, atque etiam Facultatum quae sunt pro Religiosis Familiis quibuslibet, reservantur Sacrae Congregationi de Seminariis et Studiorum Universitatibus."

[34] Cf. Maroto, "Studia in Constitutione apost. Deus scientiarum Dominus," *Apollinaris*, IV (1931), 277; Markham, *The Sacred Congregation of Seminaries and Universities of Studies*, The Catholic University of America Canon Law Studies n. 384 (Washington, D. C.: The Catholic University of America, 1957), pp. 58-59.

and examines and sanctions the constitutions. For example, on April 19, 1925, it approved the constitutions of the Sisters of the Most Precious Blood at Aarle-Rixtel in Holland,[35] and on May 12, 1926, that of the Indian Congregation called Apostolic Carmel.[36] By decree of May 29, 1926, the Congregation established under its immediate jurisdiction the Capuchin Missionary College of Panorme, *salvis iuribus Sacrae Congregationis Negotiis Religiosorum praepositae.*[37] On March 19, 1937, the Congregation for the Propagation of the Faith published an instruction concerning the formation of native religious congregations.[38] In January 1933, the Congregation established a special commission for the examination of the decrees of the episcopal conferences and missionary synods, the constitutions of religious institutes under its jurisdiction, and the regulations of native regional seminaries.[39]

ARTICLE 2.   CANON 252, § 4.

By reason of the specific matters involved, the following are withdrawn from the competence of the Congregation for the Propagation of the Faith: matters pertaining to the faith, matrimonial causes, and general liturgical norms, all of which are reserved to the appropriate Congregations, namely, the Holy Office, Congregation for the Discipline of the Sacraments, and Congregation of Sacred Rites.

Moreover, the Congregation for the Propagation of the Faith does not have judicial powers. Anything which affects the internal forum, whether sacramental or non-sacramental, must be remitted to the Sacred Penitentiary.

> Haec autem Congregatio tenetur ad competentes Congregationes deferre negotia quae aut fidem attingunt, aut causas

[35] S.C.P.F., *approbationes,* 9 apr. 1925—*AAS,* XVIII (1926), 315.

[36] *Loc. cit.*

[37] S.C.P.F., decr. *Huic,* 29 maii 1926—*AAS,* XVIII (1926), 491-492.

[38] S.C.P.F., instr. *In terris missionum,* 19 mart. 1937—*AAS,* XXIX (1937), 275-278.

[39] *Annuario pontificio for 1940,* p. 721; Vromant, *Ius Missionariorum— Introductio et Normae Generales,* p. 13.

matrimoniales, aut generales normas circa sacrorum rituum disciplinam tradendas vel interpretandas.

A. *Congregation of the Holy Office*

The Congregation for the Propagation of the Faith must, even in cases from its own territories, refer to the Holy Office matters concerning faith and Christian doctrine, the Pauline privilege, and the impediments of disparity of cult and mixed religion, as well as dispensations from these impediments and from the Eucharistic fast for priests celebrating holy Mass.[40]

However, the Congregation for the Propagation of the Faith has decennial faculties concerning the interpellations for the Pauline privilege. The Congregation grants those faculties in virtue of the power received from the Roman Pontiff.

The present decennial faculties nn. 32, 33 [41] concern one and the same power of dispensing from the interpellation, but faculty n. 32 is restricted to ordinary cases, while faculty n. 33 permits its grantees the use of the power for extraordinary cases. Both faculties were originally imparted in Gregory XIII's constitution *Populis* issued on January 25, 1585,[42] which was intended for particular countries. Later, this constitution was to be extended to other regions where similar conditions prevail.[43] In other words, the constitution Populis was first given to determined mission areas. Then, it was extended by the Code of Canon Law (Canon 1125) to all areas in the same circumstances. Now the

---

[40] Can. 252, § 4; 247, §§ 3, 5; Pius X, const. *Sapienti consilio,* 29 iun. 1908, I, n. 1, ad 5: "Etsi peculiaris Congregatio sit constituta de disciplina Sacramentorum, nihilominus integra manet Sancti Officii facultas ea cognoscendi quae circa privilegium, uti aiunt, Paulinum, et impedimenta disparitatis cultus et mixtae religionis versantur, praeter ea quae attingunt dogmaticam de matrimonio, sicut etiam de aliis Sacramentis, doctrinam."— *AAS,* I (1909); Monin, *De Curia Romana,* p. 225.

[41] Cf. nn. 32, 33 in appendix I.

[42] The constitution can be found in the supplement to the Code under *documenta* VIII. Vromant, *De Matrimonio,* p. 320; Bouscaren-Ellis, *Canon Law* (Milwaukee: Bruce, 1957), pp. 604-605; Payen, *De Matrimonio in Missionibus ac Potissimum in Sinis Tractatus Practicus et Casus* (2. ed., 3 vols., Zi-Ka-Wei, 1933), Vol. II, n. 2410.

[43] Can. 1125.

Congregation for the Propagation of the Faith declares that the conditions for the use of the constitution are verified for all mission territories.

The present decennial faculty n. 34 permits, for a grave reason, the interpellations to be made before the Baptism of the party who intends to become a Catholic. Likewise, for a grave reason, and when it can be ascertained by a summary and extrajudicial process that the interpellations cannot be made, or that it would be useless to make them, the faculty dispenses from them entirely.

Cases concerning the truths of faith, revelation, the doctrinal and dogmatic aspects of the sacraments, etc., belong exclusively to the Holy Office which also has authority to judge certain criminal cases involving the faith.[44]

With regard to the authority to grant permission for reading and keeping of prohibited books:

(1) The Consistorial Congregation stated that the quinquennial faculties for the mission territories granted by the Congrega-

---

[44] Toso, *Commentaria Minora*, III, 53: "Quapropter eius est in primis, videre de delictis contra fidem, veluti apostasiae, haeresis, schismaticis, magiae, sortelegii, etc.; aut de delictis, quae haeresis suspicionem secum ferant, veluti est cum haereticis cooperatio aut in divinis communicatio (can. 2316); pactio ante matrimonium de prole extra Ecclesiam educanda (can 2319, § 1, n. 2); liberorum baptizatorum oblatio ministris acatholicis (*ibid.*, n. 3) eorumve traditio, uti acatholicae educentur (*ibid.*, n. 4); specierum consecratarum abiectio, ad malum finem abductio aut retentio (can. 2332); per annum, obdurato animo, in censura excommunicationis permansio (can. 2340, § 1); simoniaca sacramentorum ministratio vel receptio (can. 2371); aut de delictis, quae gravitatem prae se ferant, veluti ad turpia sollicitatio ad normam can. 904 (can. 2368) vel legis ielunii encharistici, de quo infra, ad normam can. 2322 [rather 2321] transgressio." Beste, *Introductio in Codicem*, p. 243, specifies a few more, namely: ". . . spiritismus, superstitio . . . absolutio complicis, violatio sigilli, simonia, matrimonium clerici, adhaesio sectae massonicae vel alii societati prohibitae." Cf. Blat, *Commentarium Textus Codicis Iuris Canonici* (5 vols., Romae, 1921), II, n. 237; De Meester, *Iuris Canonici et Iuris Canonico-civilis Compendium*, II, 77; Sipos, *Enchiridion Iuris Canonici*, p. 207; Vermeersch-Creusen, *Epitome Iuris Canonici*, I, 295; S.C.P.F., litt. encycl. 25 iul. 1883—*Coll. S.C.P.F.*, II, n. 1604: ". . . cum addito quod remittant ad S. Officium, per medium S.C. de Prop. Fide in epistola clausa, ..." (Circa facultatem Vicariorum Apostolicorum excipiendi denuntiationem in materia sollicitationis.)

tion for the Propagation of the Faith remained in effect.[45]
Among them was the *facultas tenendi et legendi libros prohibitos*
(formula I, n. 21).[46]

(2) The Consistorial Congregation furthermore permitted the
Congregation for the Propagation of the Faith to grant, as had
been done previously, the usual privileges to missionaries, including an ample permission to read prohibited books.[47] These two
decrees issued by the Consistorial Congregation gave substantially the same faculties as are conferred by the Congregation for
the Propagation of the Faith today. The following is the pertinent text.[48]

> The faculty of granting for not more than three years per-
> mission to read or keep, with precautions, however, lest they
> fall into the hands of other persons, forbidden books and
> papers, excepting works which professedly advocate heresy
> or schism, or which attempt to undermine the very founda-
> tions of religion, or which are professedly obscene; the per-
> mission to be granted to their own subjects individually,
> and only with discrimination and for just and reasonable
> cause (cf. can. 1402, § 2), that is, to such persons only as
> really need to read the said books and papers, either in
> order to refute them, or in the exercise of their own lawful
> functions, or in the pursuit of a lawful course of studies.

The Holy Office is exclusively competent in cases involving a
substantial defect in the rite of ordination,[49] and in regard to
anything that concerns the Eucharistic fast of the priest cele-
brant of holy Mass.[50]

[45] S.C. Consist., *Dubia de competentia*, IV, 12 nov. 1908—*AAS*, I (1909),
pp. 149, 151.

[46] Grentrup, "Die rechtlichen Beziehungen der Missionsländer zur römischen Kurie in der Gegenwart," *Archiv für katholisches Kirchenrecht*,
XCIII (1913), 285.

[47] Grentrup, *loc. cit.;* S.C. Consist., *Dubia de competentia*, III, 12 nov.
1908—*AAS*, I (1909), pp. 149, 151.

[48] Cf. n. 62 in appendix I. The translation is from Bouscaren, *Digest*,
IV, 69-70.

[49] Can. 1993, § 1; S.C. Sacr., decr. 9 iun. 1931—*AAS*, XXIII (1931), 457;
Pius X, const. *Sapienti consilio*, 29 iun. 1908, n. 3, ad 3—*AAS*, I (1909),
11; Bouscaren, *Digest*, I, 812.

[50] Can. 247, § 5.

B. *Congregation for the Discipline of the Sacraments*

The Congregation for the Discipline of the Sacraments is in charge of general supervision in disciplinary matters affecting the seven sacraments, except in those things which are reserved to the Holy Office [51] and to the Congregation of Sacred Rites.[52]

Canon 249, § 2, states that it pertains to the Congregation to make decisions and to grant dispensations in matters pertaining to matrimonial discipline, the discipline of the other sacraments, and the celebration of the holy Mass, with the exception of those matters which are reserved to the other Congregations. One of these exceptions is made in favor of the Congregation for the Propagation of the Faith in virtue of the decennial faculties granted to it for certain mission territories. The *formulae* of the decennial faculties are granted by the Congregation in virtue of the power received from the Roman Pontiff.[53]

Canon 249, § 3, declares that the Congregation for the Discipline of the Sacraments also has exclusive competence over establishing the fact of the nonconsummation of marriage, and the existence of causes militating in favor of dispensation, as well as over all related points. Also questions of the validity of marriage, sacred orders, and other sacraments may be brought before this Congregation, which, according to its own judgment, may turn the cases over to the Roman Rota.

In regions subject to the Congregation for the Propagation of the Faith, the Congregation for the Discipline of the Sacraments is competent only in matrimonial cases.[54] Nevertheless, the former does in fact have the faculties for certain matrimonial dispensations, *sanatio in radice*, and the legitimation of children.[55]

The present decennial faculty n. 29 allows one to dispense

[51] Can. 247, §§ 3, 5.

[52] Can. 249, §§ 1, 2.

[53] Cf. *Periodica*, XLIX (1960), 341-352.

[54] Can. 252, § 4.

[55] Wernz-Vidal, *Ius Canonicum*, Vol. V, n. 615; McDevitt, *Legitimacy and Legitimation*, The Catholic University of America Canon Law Studies, n. 138 (Washington, D. C.: The Catholic University of America Press, 1941), pp. 192-193.

from all the impediments of ecclesiastical law,[56] regardless of whether they are diriment or prohibitive, major or minor, public or occult, and even though they are multiple. The three impediments of ecclesiastical law, as stated in the text of the faculty itself, are lack of the age required, i.e., fourteen completed years in males, twelve in females; [57] the impediments arising from the order of priesthood; [58] and affinity in the direct line if the marriage from which the affinity arose was consummated.[59]

Impediments which do not come under the decennial faculty are those of the divine and the natural law, i.e., impotency,[60] ligamen,[61] consanguinity in every degree of the direct line and in the first degree of the collateral line.[62]

The present decennial faculty n. 30 allows one to grant a *sanatio in radice* for a marriage null and void by reason of the presence of the defect of the prescribed form or of any impediment of ecclesiastical law stated above in faculty n. 29. It does grant *sanatio in radice* of marriages the invalidity of which is a matter of the external forum, except when the impediments of disparity of cult and mixed religion are concerned. The faculty calls attention to Canons 1133-1141.[63] The offspring, with the exception of adulterine and sacrilegious, born or conceived by the parties in question are legitimated *ex tunc,* i.e., from the time the marriage was contracted, although the marriage becomes valid only at the moment when the *sanatio in radice* is granted.[64]

The present decennial faculty n. 31 deals with a case of an attempt at a mixed marriage when the parties have appeared be-

[56] Can. 1058-1064; 1070-1080.

[57] Can. 1067, § 1.

[58] Can. 1072.

[59] Can. 1077.

[60] Can. 1068.

[61] Can. 1069.

[62] Can. 1076.

[63] Cf. n. 29, appendix I.

[64] Can. 1138, § 1; 1051.

fore a non-Catholic minister or a civil magistrate and the marriage is invalid because of the defect of the prescribed form. This faculty can be used, as long as it is morally certain that the non-Catholic party will not impede the Catholic education of the children which will be born to the couple.[65]

In judicial matters involving the validity or invalidity [66] of the marriage bond (nullity cases), the tribunals of the Holy See are competent to the exclusion of the Congregation for the Discipline of the Sacraments and the Congregation for the Propagation of the Faith, if in fact these cases are brought to the Holy See.[67]

All other questions of matrimonial cases, besides those for which the Congregation for the Propagation of the Faith grants faculties in virtue of the power received from the Roman Pontiff, are exclusively in the competence of the Congregation for the Discipline of the Sacraments, even in regions subject to the former, e.g., a dispensation for non-consummated marriages [68] and other questions and cases.[69]

In cases affecting the other sacraments, the Congregation for the Propagation of the Faith remains competent to exercise its authority in territories subject to its jurisdiction, even over matters reserved to the Congregation for the Discipline of the Sacraments for the rest of the world.[70]   Thus, the discipline relating to the other six sacraments, to the time, to the place, and to the conditions prescribed for the celebration of Mass, to the recep-

[65] Cf. n. 31, appendix I.

[66] S.C. Sacr. decr. *Provida,* 15 aug. 1936—*AAS,* XXVIII (1936), 314-361; Bouscaren, *Digest,* II, 471-530.

[67] Can. 1576, § 1; S.C. Consist., *Romana,* 28 ian. 1909—*AAS,* I (1909), 211.

[68] S.C. Sacr. decr. *Catholica doctrina,* 7 maii 1923—*AAS,* XV (1923), 389-413; Bouscaren, *Digest,* I, 765-792.

[69] The presumed death of a spouse (can. 1069, § 2) and the cases concerning the separation of consorts (can. 1128-1132) may be either administrative or judicial.

[70] Without prejudice to the rights of the Congregation for the Oriental Church, according to the *motu proprio Sancta Dei ecclesia* of Pius XI, on March 25, 1938—*AAS,* XXX (1938), 154-159; Bouscaren, *Digest,* II, 111-114.

tion of the holy Communion and the reservation of the Blessed Sacrament in places subject to the Congregation for the Propagation of the Faith, belongs to the same Congregation.

C. *Congregation of Sacred Rites*

Matters which proximately concern sacred rites and ceremonies are within the competence of the Congregation of Sacred Rites. These include liturgical books, new Offices, calendars, resolution of doubts, rubrics prescribed for the celebration of the holy Mass, administration of the sacraments, other services of the Latin Church, and the correct interpretation and the observance of these norms. The Congregation of Sacred Rites also grants dispensations, honorary insignia, and privileges referring to rites and ceremonies, and corrects abuses that may occur in all these matters.[71]

In regard to such cases elsewhere proper to the Congregation of Sacred Rites, the same power is exercised by the Congregation for the Propagation of the Faith for its subjects, unless general norms are involved.[72] According to Canon 252, § 4, the latter must leave to the Congregation of Sacred Rites anything concerning the general liturgical norms to be enacted, interpreted, etc. In other cases, the Congregation for the Propagation of the Faith may act.[73]

The law of the constitution *Sapienti consilio* of Pius X in 1908 granted such powers to the Congregation for the Propagation of the Faith,[74] and this was confirmed by a decision of the Consistorial Congregation in 1909.[75] Finally, it was incorporated un-

---

[71] Can. 253, §§ 1, 2.

[72] Cf. can. 252, § 4.

[73] Cf. Toso, *Commentaria Minora*, II, 63: "Scilicet ea tantum nos quod attinet et post promulgationem Codicis, Congregatio de Prop. Fide ad S. Rituum Congregationem deferre debet, quae attingunt normas generales (id est leges) liturgicas constituendas vel interpretandas; cetera per se ipsa expedire potest."

[74] Pius X, const. *Sapienti consilio*, I, 29 iun. 1908, n. 6, ad 4—*AAS*, I (1909), 12.

[75] S.C. Consist., *Dubia de competentia*, 7 ian. 1909, IV—*AAS*, I (1909), 149, 151: "Cum Sacra Congregatio de Propaganda teneatur deferre ad

changed in Canon 252, § 4.

ARTICLE 3. CANON 252, § 5.

What is the authority of the Congregation for the Propagation of the Faith over the members of religious institutes? Until 1908, it exercised power over them in many instances, and all institutes which were under its jurisdiction had to apply to the Congregation for approbation.[76]

The constitution *Sapienti consilio* changed and restricted this power of the Congregation for the Propagation of the Faith to cases pertaining to the religious as missionaries. In cases affecting them as religious, on the other hand, the Congregation for Religious alone is competent.[77] Consequently, the former has no power over the internal discipline of the various religious orders and congregations.[78] This certainly holds true of the older orders and congregations whose members are in the missions, but certain religious congregations, even after the promulgation of the Code, are in fact subject to the Congregation for the Propagation of the Faith, and this even in regard to their internal religious discipline.[79]

Sanctam Congregationem Rituum 'quaecumque attingunt sacrorum rituum disciplinam,' quaeritur, utrum hoc praescriptum respiciat rituum disciplinam prout ipsa determinatur ac circumscribitur a Constitutione Sapienti consilio, an extendatur quoque ad facultates Missam, divinum Officium aliaque spectantes, quas ante largiri consueverant sive Congregatio Rituum sive etiam Congregatio de Propaganda. Ad IV. Affirmative ad primam partem, negative ad secundam."

[76] Colomiatti, *Codex Iuris Pontificii seu Canonici* (3 vols., Vol. I—pt. 1-3; pt. 4-5, Taurini, 1888-1906), I, 897; Vincente, *Recentia Instituta* (Madrid, 1916), n. 51. The Congregation for the Propagation of the Faith also settled the important question concerning the nature of the vows of religious orders in the United States. Cf. *ASS*, I (1865), 709-712.

[77] Pius X, const. *Sapienti consilio*, 29 iun. 1908, I, n. 6, ad 5—*AAS*, I (1909), 12. *Fontes*, n. 682, ad 5; can. 252, § 5.

[78] Pius X, const. *Sapienti consilio*, 29 iun. 1908, I, n. 6, ad 5—*AAS*, I (1909), 12. *Sylloge*, n. 9; Ojetti, *De Curia Romana*, n. 74; Vromant, *De Personis*, p. 14.

[79] Stanghetti, *Prassi*, p. 19: "Anche per quanto riguarda la disciplina interna religiosa."

Canon 252, § 5, repeats word for word the rule of the constitution *Sapienti consilio*.

> Quod vero spectat ad sodales religiosos, eadem Congregatio sibi vindicat quidquid religiosos qua missionarios, sive uti singulos sive simul sumptos, tangit. Quidquid vero religiosos qua tales, sive uti singulos sive simul sumptos attingit, ad Congregationem religiosorum negotiis praepositam remittat aut relinquat.

A. *Jurisdiction over Religious Institutes*

In principle, the authority of the Congregation for the Propagation of the Faith affects religious only in their capacity as missionaries, either as individuals or as a body. The Congregation for Religious is competent for religious as religious, i.e., for everything which refers to their government, state, discipline, studies, property, privileges, and exemption.[80]

With regard to the erection of religious houses, the permission of the Holy See, accorded through the Congregation for the Propagation of the Faith, and written consent of the local ordinary are required in mission regions. There must be a question, however, of the erection of a true religious house. Very often religious in mission territories occupy houses which are not intended to be such. Thus, two or three members of a community may be sent to direct schools, infirmaries, or mission stations, but remain attached to a larger community whose superior is also their proper and immediate local superior.[81] These houses may be erected with the authorization of the local ordinary alone.[82] The reason for demanding Roman approbation of the erection of a true and distinct religious house in mission territories is the desire of the Holy See for an orderly and uniform regime with respect to religious life in these regions.[83]

---

[80] *Normae peculiares*, cap. I, ad e—*AAS*, I (1909), 60; can. 251, § 1.

[81] Schäfer, *De Religiosis ad Normam Codicis Iuris Canonici* (3. ed., Romae, 1940), n. 80; Vermeersch-Creusen, *Epitome Iuris Canonici*, Vol. I, n. 560; can. 497, § 1: Larraona, "Commentarium Codicis," *CpRM*, V (1924), 423.

[82] Cf. can. 497, § 3.

[83] S.C.P.F., litt. 7 dec. 1901—*ASS*, XXIV (1901-1902), 639.

With regard to papal approval of institutes, it is evident from Canon 252, § 5, that religious institutes have to apply to the Congregation for Religious for such approbation, even if they are founded in a mission land subject to the Congregation for the Propagation of the Faith and, outside mission territory, even if this scope is purely missionary. Certainly, papal approval concerns religious institutes as religious, since the precise purpose of this approval is to pass judgment on the religious life and to confer religious status on the institute. Moreover, those institutes which had previously been approved by the Congregation for the Propagation of the Faith now come under the jurisdiction of the Congregation for Religious.[84]

In practice, this change concerning competence did not produce the best results. The Congregation for the Propagation of the Faith has actually approved certain missionary congregations since the promulgation of the Code. Thus, in 1921 it approved the Congregation of the Missionaries of the B. V. Mary of Scheut and this institute was placed under its jurisdiction by a special decree.[85] The same favor was granted to the Missionary Canoneses of St. Augustine (*Canonissae missionariae a Sancto Augustino*), in Belgium on October 1, 1926, as well as to many other institutes which will be listed later.[86] These religious institutes are subject to the Congregation even as regards internal discipline in spite of Canon 252, § 5.[87]

Such special arrangements in particular instances may gradually effect a change to the extent that the Congregation for the Propagation of the Faith receives power over purely mis-

---

[84] S.C. Consist., *Dubia de competentia*, V, 7 ian. 1909—*AAS*, I (1909), 149, 151, ad. V: "Etiam quoad Congregationes religiosas, quarum regulas seu constitutiones approbatae sunt a Congregatione de Propaganda, standum praescriptis Constitutionis Sapienti consilio"; Ojetti, *Synopsis Rerum Moralium et Iuris Pontificii* (Romae, 1911), Vol. II, n. 3348.

[85] S.C.P.F., decr. 18 mart. 1921—*AAS*, XIII (1921), 354.

[86] Vromant, *Ius Missionariorum*, p. 13; Ojetti, *De Curia Romana*, n. 74.

[87] S.C.P.F., decr. 18 mart. 1921—*AAS*, XIII (1921), 354: ". . . etiam in iis quae spectant ad internam religiosam disciplinam, iurisdictioni huius S.C. de Propaganda Fide."

sionary institutes.[88]   The law, however, is not changed in this matter.   Instead particular concessions have been tolerated and allowed by the Holy See.[89]

There seems to be no reason why a similar jurisdiction should not govern all religious institutes which have for their purpose missionary activities subject to the Congregation for the Propagation of the Faith.   If there is any reason for maintaining the contrary, it would be to bring about unity of rule for all religious under one Roman Congregation.   Yet the concessions made, thus far are particular ones and apply only to the cases mentioned. Consequently, it cannot be said that the Congregation for the Propagation of the Faith has the right to approve all missionary institutes.   Whenever an institute approaches the Holy See for any degree of approbation, it should apply to the Congregation for Religious, since the law of the Code has not been abrogated.

Notwithstanding various restrictions imposed on its competence by Pius X and his successors, it is obvious that the Congregation for the Propagation of the Faith retains and exercises considerable jurisdiction.   It enjoys for its territories and its subjects most of the powers which are shared by the other Roman Congregations in relation to other territories.   In practice, the individuals who come under its jurisdiction may address themselves to the Congregation in all matters.   If the matter does not pertain to its competence, the Congregation will undertake to forward the request to the appropriate authority.

B. *Religious Congregations under the Authority of the Congregation*

In the case of religious institutes with members of either sex, either in mission lands or outside them, which pursue an exclusively missionary purpose and are in fact dependent on the Congregation for the Propagation of the Faith, this Congregation

---

[88] Ojetti, *loc. cit.*: "Missionarii qua religiosi, inde ab edita Constitutione piana *Sapienti consilio,* pendent quoque, sicut ceteri religiosi, a S.C. Religiosorum.   Quaedam tamen exceptiones, ex particulari concessione S. Sedis, decursu temporum fuerunt iterum toleratae."

[89] Vromant, *op. cit.*, p. 12.

exercises *per analogiam iuris* the same powers and faculties which the Congregation for Religious has in relation to other religious institutes and other members.[90]   Consequently, all members of the religious institutes which depend upon the Congregation for the Propagation of the Faith are under the jurisdiction of the same Congregation as religious as well as missionaries.

If the religious institutes are of pontifical approval, the Congregation deals with the establishment of institutions and provinces, the revision and approval of constitutions, the revision and approval of missionary statutes,[91] examination of the quinquennial report,[92] rescripts of different kinds, dispensations, indulgences, privileges, temporal goods, studies, etc., with the exception of juridical cases and matters pertaining to the competence of the Holy Office.[93]

Within the limits of its own competence, the Congregation for the Propagation of the Faith, thus, may issue norms, instructions, decrees, and rescripts which it considers opportune to regulate the religious life of the institutes.   This Congregation enjoys the same authority in these matters as the Congregation for Religious.[94]

Negatively, a norm given by the Congregation for Religious does not oblige religious congregations dependent on the Congregation for the Propagation of the Faith, unless it explicitly states this obligation.   For example, the instruction concerning students of seminaries to be thoroughly tested before being promoted for orders was extended through the instruction given by the Congregation for Religious in 1931 to the religious clerical students of its own subjects.[95]   In 1941, the Congregation for the Propagation of the Faith issued the same instruction for its sub-

---

[90] Paventi, *Breviarium Iuris Missionalis,* p. 180; Stanghetti, *Prassi,* p. 21.

[91] Stanghetti, *Prassi,* p. 21.

[92] Can. 510.

[93] Can. 247, § 5; cf. can. 251.

[94] Paventi, *op. cit.,* p. 180.

[95] S.C. Rel., instr. 12 febr. 1931—*AAS,* XXIV (1932), 74-81.   Cf. S.C. Sacr., instr. 27 dec. 1930—*AAS,* XXIII (1931), 120-127.

jects.[96]   However, the decree concerning admission of ex-religious to a seminary or of an ex-seminarian to a religious institute, issued by the Congregation for Religious and the Congregation for Seminaries and Universities, was not extended to the subjects of the Congregation for the Propagation of the Faith.[97]

With regard to religious congregations of diocesan right, a great number of such religious congregations developed in mission lands after the promulgation of the Code.   There are also a few other diocesan congregations which, though located in places outside mission territories, for instance, the Medical Mission Sisters of the Archdiocese of Philadelphia in the United States, the Medical Missionaries of Mary of the Diocese of Armagh in Ireland, etc., have an exclusively missionary purpose.   They fall, therefore, under the juridiction of the Congregation for the Propagation of the Faith.[98]

In its directive issued on September 8, 1896 to the Vicars Apostolic of East India, the Congregation recommended the establishment in the mission of religious institutes of diocesan right for men, but only after the formation of a native clergy.[99] A more explicit recommendation of this kind was made later by Pius XI in the encyclical *Rerum ecclesiae.*[100]

On March 19, 1937, the Congregation for the Propagation of the Faith issued a special directive for the establishment of

[96] Archives S.C.P.F., prot. n. 411/41; 119/41; 2/41, cited by Paventi, *op. cit.,* p. 181, footnote n. 3.

[97] S.C. Rel., and S.C. Sem. et Stud. Univ., decr. 25 iul. 1941—*AAS,* XXX (1941), 371.

[98] Stanghetti, *Prassi,* p. 21; can. 492, § 2.

[99] S.C.P.F., instr. 8 sept. 1869—*Coll. S.C.P.F.,* II, n. 1346, ad 6: "In multis vero Vicariatibus, in quibus Religiosa Instituta vel omnino adhuc extant, vel tantum paucos sectatores habent, optimum erit consilium Vicariorum App. si, cum clero, indigenae seculari efformando operam dederint, etiam Regulares Ordines et Congregationes inter indigenas statuere satagant . . ." Cf. S.C.P.F., instr. 18 oct. 1883—*Coll. S.C.P.F.,* II, n. 1606, VII: "Neque minorem curam Vicarii App. impendant necesse est ad ea excolenda Instituta quae religiosas mulieres respiciunt."

[100] S.C.P.F., litt. encycl. *Rerum ecclesiae,* 28 febr. 1926—*AAS,* XVIII (1926), 65-83; *Sylloge,* n. 120.

native religious institutes of diocesan right for men and for women.[101]　In general, it followed the provisions issued by the Congregation for Religious in 1924.[102]　Practice, however, showed that these provisions were inadequate.　Consequently, the directive *De Regimine Congregationum (Sororum)* was issued by the Congregation for the Propagation of the Faith.[103]　Finally, the *Normae pro Constitutionibus Congregationum iuris diocesani a S.C.D.P.F. dependentium* was published in Rome on June 29, 1940.[104]　Such religious congregations of diocesan right must resort to the Congregation for the Propagation of the Faith only in a few cases, e.g., changes in wills,[105] permission to contract debts beyond a certain amount, review of the constitution, erection of a religious house in countries subject to the Congregation, and, in certain cases, granting of indulgences and dispensations from canonical prescriptions of the common law.[106]

C. *Enumeration of Religious Congregations Dependent upon the Congregation*

The following religious congregations fall under the jurisdiction of the Congregation for the Propagation of the Faith: [107]

a. Religious congregations of men of pontifical approval: [108]

1. Consolata Society for Foreign Missions (S.C. Consist., decr. 8 ian. 1919).
2. Sons of Sacred Heart of Jesus (S.C.P.F., decr. 14 iul. 1919).

[101] S.C.P.F., instr. *In terris missionum*, 19 mart. 1937—*AAS*, XXIX, (1939), 275-278.

[102] S.C. Rel., instr. 6 febr. 1924—*AAS*, XVI (1924), 96, 192, 373, 404; cf. S.C. Rel., decr. *Quod iam*, 30 nov. 1922—*AAS*, XIV (1922), 644.

[103] *Sylloge*, n. 205.　No date appears and it cannot be found in *AAS*.

[104] Stanghetti, *Prassi*, p. 29, footnote n. 10.

[105] Can. 583, n. 2.

[106] Stanghetti, *Prassi*, pp. 21-22.

[107] Stanghetti, *Prassi*, pp. 20-21; Paventi, *Breviarium Iuris Missionalis*, pp. 182-188; *Annuario Pontificio* for 1960, pp. 892-896, 912.

[108] Can. 488, n. 2.

3. Missionary Congregation of Sacred Heart of Jesus (united with the preceding institution by decree of S.C.P.F., on 27 iul. 1923).
4. Congregation of the Missionaries of Mariannhill (S.C. P.F., decr. 28 iun. 1920).
5. Pius Society of St. Francis Xavier for Foreign Missions (S.C. Rel., litt. 23 iun. 1920).
6. Congregation of the Immaculate Heart of Mary (Scheut Fathers; S.C.P.F., decr. 18 mart. 1921).
7. Congregation of the Missionaries of St. Francis of Assisi (S.C. Rel., litt. 12 aug. 1926).

b. Religious congregations of women of pontifical approval:
1. Francisan Missionaries of Mary (pontifical rescr. 7 febr. 1916).
2. Missionary Sisters of the Precious Blood (S.C.P.F., rescr. 30 dec. 1918).
3. Sodalities of St. Peter Claver (Secr. Status, rescr. 8 nov. 1919).
4. White Sisters (Missionariae Nostrae Dominae Africae vulgo Suore Bianche; S.C.P.F., rescr. 8 dec. 1940).
5. Missionary Canonesses of St. Augustine in Belgium (S. C. Rel., litt. 7 sept. 1920).
6. Pious Mothers for Negros (Piae Matres a Nigritia; S.C.P.F., rescr. 22 nov. 1920).
7. Benedictine Sisters of Tutzing (S.C.P.F., rescr. 30 iun. 1922).
8. Sisters of the Third Order of St. Dominic: of Kingwilliamstown, of Salisbury, of Oakford (S.C.P.F., litt. 21 nov. 1923).
9. Sisters of Our Lady of the Apostles (Sorores N. Dominae Apostolorum; S.C.P.F., decr. 7 aug. 1922).
10. Sister Servants of the Holy Ghost (S.C.P.F., rescr. 20 ian. 1923).
11. Missionary Sisters of the Holy Ghost (S.C.P.F., decr. 22 mart. 1923).
12. Apostolic Carmel for India (S.C. Rel., litt. 18 nov. 1924).

13. Missionary Sisters of Society of Mary (S.C.P.F., decr. 30 dec. 1931).
14. Missionary Sisters of the Consolata (S.C.P.F., decr. 15 maii 1930).
15. Little Servants of the Sacred Heart (S.C.P.F., decr. 8 iul. 1935).
16. Salvatorian Sisters (Ordo Sororum Ssmi. Salvatoris et S. Birgitae; S.C.P.F., decr. 2 dec. 1942).
17. Japanese Sisters of the Visitation (S.C.P.F., decr. 18 dec. 1942).
18. Missionary Sisters Congregation of the Queen of Apostles (S.C.P.F., decr. 8 apr. 1949).
19. Congregation of Daughters of the Sacred Heart of Jesus (S.C.P.F., decr. 7 apr. 1949).
20. Third Order Apostolic of Our Lady of Carmel of Trivanto (Tertius Ordo Apost. Nostrae Dominae a Carmelo de Trivandrum; S.C.P.F., decr. 7 febr. 1950).
21. Third Order of Our Lady of Mount Carmel and St. Theresa of Verapoly (Tertius Ordo N. Dominae a Monte Carmelo et a S. Teresia de Verapoly; S.C.P.F., decr. 15 febr. 1951).

c. Religious congregation of diocesan approval erected outside mission territory in place of common law.[109]
1. Pious Sister Servants of the Sacred Heart (diocese of Nice, France; decr. 24 apr. 1933).
2. Sisters for Foreign Missions (diocese of Toulouse, France; decr. 8 mart. 1933).
3. Dominican Sisters of Namur (diocese of Namur, Belgium; decr. 21 nov. 1937).
4. Medical Missionaries of Mary (diocese of Armagh, Ireland; decr. 21 mart. 1940).
5. Medical Mission Sisters (archdiocese of Philadelphia, U.S.A.; litt. Secr. Status, 30 decr. 1941).
6. Sons of Mary Health of the Sick (archdiocese of Boston, U.S.A.: litt. S.C.P.F., 24 mart. 1954).[110]

---

[109] Stanghetti, *Prassi*, p. 21.

[110] By private communication.

Besides these institutes, there are many congregations of diocesan right for men and women erected in mission territories themselves. These, of course, come under the jurisdiction of the Congregation for the Propagation of the Faith.

Finally, the Congregation has established a particular commission of consultors, the *Commissio super revisione synodorum et conferentiarum episcoporum, constitutionum Institutorum religiosorum a S.C.P.F. dependentium et regularium Seminariorum regionalium indigenarum.* Among other things the title of this commission indicates that its work includes the examination of constitutions of religious institutes.[111]

[111] Cf. Paventi, *Breviarium Iuris Missionalis,* p. 181.

CHAPTER VI

PRESENT INDIRECT COMPETENCE OF THE OTHER CONGREGATIONS

Article 1. Roman Congregations

Until the beginning of the XXth century, the Congregation for the Propagation of the Faith remained the only pontifical body immediately exercising the authority of the Roman Pontiff in missionary affairs. At its foundation, in 1622, it was entrusted by Gregory XV with the whole organization and direction of the Catholic apostolate in the world of infidelity, schism, and heresy.

Since the issuance of the constitution *Sapienti consilio,* the missionary administration of the Congregation for the Propagation of the Faith is no longer so complete or extensive. Other Congregations share this, although matters affecting the missions are handled in very unequal degrees and not by all the Roman dicasteries. Next the rôle of the other Congregations in the organization and the government of the missions needs to be considered.

A. *Congregation for the Oriental Church*

On June 6, 1862, Pius IX established the *Congregatio de Propaganda Fide pro negotiis ritus orientalis* within the Congregations for the Propagation of the Faith. At this time, he divided the latter into two distinct sections under one Cardinal Prefect, each with its own personnel, secretariat, and proper archives.[1]

The purpose of the new Congregation was to protect the rites and discipline proper to Orientals and to guard against any elements contrary to the Catholic faith and dangerous to the salvation of souls. Rite in the canonical sense has a wider comprehension than the liturgical sense. It includes not only liturgical matters, but also the entire body of law, the whole discipline of a determined group of the faithful, which is fully acknowl-

---

[1] Pius IX, const. *Romani pontifices,* 6 iun. 1862—*Coll. S.C.P.F.,* I, n. 1223.

edged by the Holy See as independent, autonomous, *sui iuris*.[2]
The Oriental rites are distinguished by such elements as variety
of disciplinary observance, rites for celebration of worship, and
especially grouping under the jurisdiction of ecclesiastical superiors who are independent of one another.[3] The *Congregatio de
Propaganda Fide pro negotiis ritus orientalis* handled all the
affairs of Orientals, even mixed matters which by reason of matter or persons affect Latin Catholics, unless it was obliged to refer
such matters to the Congregation fo the Propagation of the
Faith.[4]

Although constant efforts were made by the Congregation for the
Propagation of the Faith to harmonize activities of missionaries of
the Latin rite and those of the Oriental rites,[5] the situation some-
times presented serious dangers and caused regrettable frictions.
Too many missionaries of Latin rite, misquoting the decrees of
the Congregation for the Propagation of the Faith, suggested by
their actions and attitudes that the reign of Christ was to be
identified with the Latin forms of religious life and sought the
elimination of cultural diversity as a necessary means to Catholic unity. The missionaries of the Latin Church were much attached to their own traditions, and were easily suspicious, while
the Orientals assumed a corresponding attitude of opposition.[6]

Many Orientals considered their situation to be one of inferior-
ity and felt that it was a somewhat humiliating subjection to the
Congregation for the Propagation of the Faith, the supreme
direction of which belonged to Latins.[7]

[2] Wojnar, "The Code of Oriental Canon Law, De Ritibus Orientalibus
and De Personis," *The Jurist*, XIX (1959), 278.

[3] V. Martin, *Les Congrégations Romaines*, pp. 196-197.

[4] Pius IX, const. *Romani pontifices*, 6 iun. 1862—*Coll. S.C.P.F.*, I, n.
1223—*Fontes*, n. 531: "Nova Congregatio a Nobis instituta omnia orientalium negotia, etiamsi mixta, quae scilicet sive rei, sive personarum ratione
latinos attingant, tractare debebit, nisi eadem Congregatio negotia ipsa ad
generalem Propagandae Fidei Congregationem deferenda esse interdum
existimaverit."

[5] S.C.P.F., instr. 23 sept. 1783—*Coll. S.C.P.F.*, I, n. 565.

[6] V. Martin, *Les Congrégations Romaines*, pp. 193-194.

[7] *Loc. cit.*

Benedict XV decided to separate the Congregation for the Oriental Churches completely from the Congregation for the Propagation of the Faith and to hold the office of Prefect of the former personally. The separation was decreed on May 1, 1917, and the Congregation began its work on December 1, 1917.[8] The norms of the *motu proprio Dei providentis*, by which this was effected, were incorporated substantially into Canon 257 of the Code. This confers on the Congregation for the Oriental Church very extensive jurisdiction over the churches of its competence. Without prejudice to the rights of the Holy Office and those of the Sacred Penitentiary for the internal forum, it exercises, with regard to its own subjects, all powers possessed by the other Roman Congregations for the churches of the Latin rite.[9]

Notwithstanding this determination of the competence of the Congregation for the Oriental Church, however, the special religious situation of the countries depending upon the Congregation presented, at least for twenty years after the Code, a twofold anomaly. First, the Congregation for the Propagation of the Faith still exercised its jurisdiction over the priests, monks and nuns, and the faithful of the Latin rite in these places, apart from mixed questions. Second, the apostolic works of all kinds of the Latin missionaries presented in fact mixed characteristics, e.g., the hospitals, dispensaries, clinics, and schools which were conducted by the Latin missionaries admitted Orientals of all rites, etc.[10]

As already indicated, according to the successive decisions of Pius IX, Benedict XV, and the Code of Canon Law, mixed mat-

---

[8] Benedict XV, motu propr. *Dei providentis*, 1 maii 1917—*AAS*, IX (1917), 529-531; *Fontes*, n. 710.

[9] Can. 257, § 2; Benedict XV, motu propr. *Dei providentis*, 1 maii 1917— *AAS*, IX (1917), 531 ad IV; *Sylloge*, n. 56, ad IV: "Pro Ecclesiis ritus orientalis haec Congregatio omnibus facultatibus potitur, quae aliae Congregationes pro Ecclesiis ritus latini obtinent, salvo tamen iure Congregationis Sancti Officii."

[10] Creusen, "Motu proprio sur la jurisdiction de la S. Congregation de l'Eglise Orientale," *Nouvelle Revue Theologique*, LXV (1939), 983-984; Staffa, "De Sacrae Congregationis pro Ecclesia Orientali Competentia," *Apollinaris*, XI (1938), 361-363; Pius XI, motu propr. *Sancta Dei ecclesia*, 25 mart. 1938—*AAS*, XXX (1938), 155.

ters (*negotia mixta*) which by reason of the thing or of the person affect Latins pertain to the exclusive competence of the Congregation for the Oriental Church.[11] The latter's jurisdiction, however, did not extend to other cases concerning persons of the Latin rite found in Oriental countries.[12] This caused an abnormal situation to which Pius XI brought an effective and final remedy.

In his *motu proprio Sancta Dei ecclesia* of March 25, 1938, Pius XI completely suppressed the competence of the Congregation for the Propagation of the Faith in all territories where Orientals form the great majority of the Christian population.[13] Thus, for example, Southern Albania was placed under the jurisdiction of the Congregation for the Oriental Church, but Northern Albania was not affected. In the latter case, both the Congregation for the Propagation of the Faith and the Congregation for the Oriental Church retained their jurisdiction.[14] In anticipation of the *motu proprio Sancta Dei ecclesia,* both Eritrea and Northern Ethiopia had already been placed under the exclusive jurisdiction of the Oriental Church.[15]

By force of the *motu proprio* of Pius XI, many countries passed gradually under the full and exclusive competence of the Congregation for the Oriental Church. The following is the pertinent text.[16]

[11] Can. 257, § 1.

[12] Benedict XV, motu propr. *Dei providentis,* 1 maii 1917—*AAS,* IX (1917), 529. Cf. Bouscaren, *Digest,* II, 114.

[13] Pius XI, motu propr. *Sancta Dei ecclesia,* 25 mart. 1938—*AAS,* XXX (1938), 157-159.

[14] Dziob, *The Sacred Congregation for the Oriental Church,* p. 126, footnote, n. 7.

[15] S.C. Orient., *nominationes,* 28 iul. 1937; 21 sept. 1937—*AAS,* XXIX (1937), 435.

[16] Pius XI, motu propr. *Sancta Dei ecclésia,* 25 mart. 1938—*AAS,* XXX (1938), 157-158. (1) On June 1, 1938: Palestine, Transjordan, Egypt, the Peninsula of Sinai and the Island of Cyprus. (2) On January 1, 1939: Greece, the Dodecanese Islands, Southern Albania, Bulgaria, Asiatic Turkey, and Thracia subject to Turkey. (3) On June 1, 1939: Syria, Lebanon, Iraq, and Iran. Cf. *Sylloge,* n. 206. The translation is from Bouscaren, *Digest,* II, 111-113.

> I. The Sacred Congregation for the Oriental Church, which is presided over by the Sovereign Pontiff himself, has full and exclusive jurisdiction over the following countries: Egypt and the Peninsula of Sinai, Eritrea and Northern Ethiopia, Southern Albania, Bulgaria, Cyprus, Greece, the Dodecanese Islands, Iran, Iraq, Lebanon, Palestine, Syria, Transjordan, Asiatic Turkey, and Thracia subject to Turkey.

So far as jurisdiction is concerned, in the territories enumerated above the Congregation for the Oriental Church has the same powers for Oriental Catholics which it enjoys everywhere. In regard to the Latin Catholics, however, the Congregation for the Propagation of the Faith surrendered only the power which it possessed according to Canon 252. Consequently, other Congregations of the Roman Curia, which had some jurisdiction over the Latin Catholics who were subject to the Congregation for the Propagation of the Faith, still retained the same authority towards them. These were Holy Office, Congregation for the Discipline of the Sacraments, Congregation of Sacred Rites, Congregation of Seminaries and Universities of Studies, and the Sacred Penitentiary:

> II. Consequently, in the above-mentioned regions this Sacred Congregation possesses, not only for the faithful of the Oriental rite but also for the faithful of the Latin rite, and for their hierarchy, works, institutes, and pious associations, all the faculties which the other Sacred Congregations possess for the faithful of the Latin rite outside these territories, without prejudice, however, to the right of the Holy Office, and without diminution of the reservations which have hitherto been made to the Sacred Congregation of the Sacraments, to the Sacred Congregation of Rites, to the Sacred Congregation of Seminaries and Universities, and to the Sacred Penitentiary.

In the other areas not included among the above-named regions, the jurisdiction of the Congregation for the Oriental Church continued to be exercised, but not in an exclusive manner, i.e., in accordance with the rights established by Canon 257: [17]

---

[17] Can. 257, § 1: "Huic Congregationi reservantur omnia cuiusque generis negotia quae sive ad personas sive ad disciplinam, sive ad ritus Ecclesiarum

III. As regards the faithful of the Oriental rite who reside outside the place aforementioned, the competency of the Sacred Congregation for the Oriental Church remains in all respects intact. To it, therefore, are reserved all matters of whatever kind which concern either the persons or the discipline or the rite of the Oriental Church, even though they be mixed, that is, though they also touch the Latins either by reason of the thing or of the person concerned; and for these faithful it has all the faculties which, for faithful of the Latin rite, belong to other Congregations, always without prejudice to the right of the Holy Office, and without diminution of the reservations which have hitherto been made to the Sacred Congregation of Seminaries and Universities and to the Sacred Penitentiary.

VII. When the countries of the Christian East will have passed under the exclusive jurisdiction of the Sacred Congregation for the Oriental Church, the documents regarding these countries, which are kept in the archives of the Sacred Congregation for the Propagation of the Faith, shall be transferred and delivered to the archives of the Sacred Congregation for the Oriental Church, as far as this is possible and according to the mutual agreement of those entrusted with these two Offices.

VIII. The Sacred Congregation for the Propagation of the Faith will hand over to the Sacred Congregation for the Oriental Church all funds which are destined for works and institutions of those countries which have been asigned to the exclusive juridiction of the latter. In case no such distinct funds exist, the Sacred Congregation for the Propagation of the Faith shall make up from its own funds a revenue equivalent to the amount of all the ordinary and extraordinary subsidies which this Sacred Congregation was accustomed to send every year to the aforesaid countries for their respective works and institutions. The extraordinary subsidies should be calculated on the average amount sent yearly to these countries in the course of the last three years, that is 1935 to 1937.

IX. The Pontifical Work of the Propagation of the Faith will yearly remit to the Sacred Congregation for the Oriental Church a sum which will maintain a fixed

---

orientalium referuntur, etiamsi sint mixta, quae scilicet sive rei sive personarum ratione latinos quoque attingant." Cf. *Sylloge,* n. 206, III.

comparative ratio and proportion between the total amount of the subsidies, both ordinary and extraordinary, which have been sent in the last three years, as has been stated, in favor of the Orientals and Latins in those countries, and the grand total of the receipts and revenues which the said Work of the Propagation of the Faith has received during the same period.

X. The Pontifical Work of Saint Peter the Apostle for the Native Clergy will yearly remit to the Sacred Congregation for the Oriental Church an amount equal to 2 per cent of all the revenues and receipts of the said Pontifical Work.

XI. The Substitute of the Sacred Congregation for the Oriental Church is a member by right of the Supreme General Council of the Pontifical Works of the Propagation of the Faith and of Saint Peter the Apostle for the Native Clergy.

In summary, by the action of Pius XI, the Congregation for the Oriental Church received competence over all Latins, clergy and faithful, including the missions and missionaries, within its territories. Thus, the Congregation for the Propagation of the Faith was deprived of competence over the Latin missions in the areas which are considered Oriental.

B. *Consistorial Congregation*

On January 22, 1588,[18] Sixtus V established the Consistorial Congregation, among other Congregations, in the constitution *Immensa aeterni Dei.*[19] It is presided over by the Roman Pontiff himself as Prefect and is the principal organ of the Apostolic See in matters concerning the government of dioceses falling under the common law. The Consistorial Congregation, as its name indicates, prepares the report of matters to be discussed at the Consistory.[20]

[18] Coronata, *Institutiones Iuris Canonici,* Vol. I, n. 329, footnote n. 5: "Constit. 'Immensa' habet revera datam 22 Ianuarii, 1587, at, quia, ante Pium X anni computabantur in datatione bullarum a die 25 Martii, seu a die Incarnationis non Nativitatis Domini, inde fit ut revera annus quo illa constitutio edita est non fuerit in communi computatione annus 1587 sed 1588." Cf. Simier, *La Curie Romaine,* p. 128, footnote n. 2.

[19] *Bull. Rom.,* VIII, 985-997.

[20] Can. 248.

The territorial jurisdiction of this Congregation includes Europe and the Americas, except for those missionary regions which depend upon the Congregation for the Propagation of the Faith. Moreover, a certain number of archdioceses and dioceses, although located in the area of missions, depend directly upon the Consistorial Congregation. These are, in Africa: the archdiocese of Carthage; the archdiocese of Algiers and its two suffragans, Constantine and Oran; the diocese of Angola and Congo, Angra, Funchal, Santiago de Capoverde, San Tommasco (all suffragans of Lisbon); the prelature *nullius* of Mozambique; the diocese of Cadiz (suffragan of Seville). In India: the patriarchate of Goa with its two suffragans, Cochin and Meliapour. In China: the diocese of Macao (suffragan of Goa).[21] In the Philippine Islands, apart from mission territories subject to the Congregation for the Propagation of the Faith, the dioceses depend upon the Consistorial Congregation.[22] Finally, it should be noted that the Consistorial Congregation effectively directs missionary activities in certain dioceses and prelatures *nullius* of Latin America, outside the regions subject to the jurisdiction of the Congregation for the Propagation of the Faith.[23]

In principle, the competence of the Consistorial Congregation does not extend to the territories of the Congregation for the Propagation of the Faith [24] or to affairs involving negotiations with civil governments, although the territories may normally be included in its jurisdiction.[25] The missionary prerogatives of the Consistorial Congregation are distinct from those of the Congregation for the Propagation of the Faith and much more limited. Nevertheless, the Consistorial Congregation has the power to elevate, in due course, the apostolic vicariates and prefectures to the status of dioceses falling under the common law. Similarly, when a diocese under its jurisdiction is reduced to a

---

[21] *AAS*, XXXII (1940), 217-244; Bouscaren, *Digest*, II, 11-24. These data are drawn from the *Annuario Pontificio* for 1960, *passim*.

[22] *Annuario Pontificio* for 1960, *passim*.

[23] *Guida*, p. 49; Champagne, *Manual of Missionary Action*, p. 67.

[24] Can. 248, § 2.

[25] Can. 255.

vicariate or prefecture, this territory will pass to the jurisdiction of Propaganda after it acquires the changed status.[26]

C. *Congregation for Extraordinary Ecclesiastical Affairs*

The Congregation for Extraordinary Ecclesiastical Affairs goes back to Pius VII who established it in 1814.[27] It is presided over by a Prefect, who is the Cardinal Secretary of State.[28] Canon Law gives this Congregation jurisdiction to treat certain matters which cannot be settled according to the norms of the administration of the Church.[29] It thus possesses the authority to create new dioceses, to divide old dioceses, and to name the respective ordinaries of these territories whenever negotiations with a civil government are required.[30] In virtue of this principle, the Congregation for Extraordinary Ecclesiastical Affairs selects the titular bishops in those mission territories where the civil government has some right to intervene, either because of a right of patronage, or by reason of a concordat or other agreement entered into with the Holy See. The examples are the regions of the Portuguese Padroado. In these cases, the ordinaries of the territories depend upon the Consistorial Congregation for spiritual faculties in spite of the powers of the Congregation for Extraordinary Ecclesiastical Affairs.[31]

In the past century, the Congregation for Extraordinary Ecclesiastical Affairs exercised a permanent jurisdiction over a certain number of strictly missionary areas, chiefly in Latin America. As long as the political power of Spain endured in Latin America, ecclesiastical affairs were handled at Madrid between the Nuncio

---

[26] S.C. Consist., decr. *Quo facilius*, 15 iul. 1932—*AAS*, XXV (1933), 206-207: "Sedem autem praefecturae apostolicae in urbe Baguio eadem Sanctitas Sua constituit. Hanc autem novam praefecturam apostolicam Sacrae Congregationis de Propaganda Fide prout de iure subiicit." Cf. S.C. Consist., decr. *Quo melius*, 5 febr. 1932—*AAS*, XXV (1933), 154-155; I (1909), 12; *Guida*, p. 48.

[27] Magnin, "La Sacrée Congrégation des Affaires Extraordinaires," *Dictionaire de Droit Canonique*, I, 546.

[28] Pius XI, *notificatio*, 5 iul. 1925—*AAS*, XVIII (1926), 89; *Guida*, p. 49.

[29] Can. 255.

[30] *AAS*, XVIII (1926), 89.

[31] *Guida*, p. 56.

and the Spanish government.[32] When the colonies first secured their independence, the Holy See continued to forward matters through the nunciature in Madrid. Later, however, the Roman Pontiff entrusted such matters to the Congregation for Extraordinary Ecclesiastical Affairs, as the respective governments protested against the manner of action of the Holy See.[33] The same occurred in certain regions which were former Portuguese colonies.[34]

After the constitution *Sapienti consilio*, the Congregation for Extraordinary Ecclesiastical Affairs continued to handle the affairs of Latin America. The vicariates and prefectures, however, over which it had authority, were transferred, without exception, to the Congregation for the Propagation of the Faith.[35]

Thus, the following now pertain to the Congregation: Lower California, in Mexico; Canelos and Macas, Mendez and Gualaquiza, Napo and Zamora, in Ecuador; Casanera, Goajira, San Martino, Interdances Orientales and Caqueta, in Colombia; Antofagasta and Rarapaca, in Chile.[36]

According to the Code of Canon Law, the Congregation for Extraordinary Ecclesiastical Affairs exercises, besides its ordinary jurisdiction, an extraordinary power conceded to it through the intermediary of the Cardinal Secretary of State, in connection with the civil laws and the agreements of the Holy See with various nations.[37]

From the point of view which is of concern here, these agreements may have a missionary character, e.g., the concordats of

[32] V. Martin, *Les Congrégations Romaines*, p. 180.

[33] *Loc. cit.*

[34] *Loc. cit.*

[35] Pius X, const. *Sapienti consilio*, 29 iun. 1908, I, n. 6, ad 3—*AAS*, I (1909), 12: "Ad eam [Propagandam] pertinere decernimus Vicariatus omnes Apostolicos, Praefecturas seu missiones quaslibet, eas quoque quae Congregationi a negotiis ecclesiasticis extraordinariis modo subsunt." Cf. Murphy, "Congregation for the Extraordinary Ecclesiastical Affairs," *The Ecclesiastical Review*, XLI (1909), 7.

[36] Pius XI, motu propr. *Sancta Dei ecclesia*, 25 mart. 1938—*AAS*, XXX (1938), 157-158. Cf. Villien, "La S. Congrégation de la Propaganda," The Canoniste Contemporain, XXXVI (1913), 510-511. *Analecta Ecclesiastica*, XI (1903), 306; XIII (1905), 417-418.

[37] Can. 255.

1857 and 1886 with Portugal; the pacts with Leopold II of Belgium for the Belgian Congo from 1906 to 1908. More often, such agreements are general but incorporate missionary matters, e.g., the concordats signed in the nineteenth century with countries of Latin America.[39] They may even contain special sections devoted to missions.[40]

Furthermore, it may be mentioned that the Congregation for Extraordinary Ecclesiastical Affairs handled strictly missionary affairs at the Peace Conference in 1919 after World War I. The official negotiator appointed by Benedict XV to protect the interests of the German Catholic missions was Msgr. Bonaventure Cerretti, the Secretary of the Congregation for Extraordinary Ecclesiastical Affairs, and not of the Congregation for the Propagation of the Faith.[41]

ARTICLE 2. REPRESENTATIVES OF THE HOLY SEE
IN MISSION COUNTRIES

The Secretary of State is aided in his work by a diplomatic staff, members of which are sent abroad in exchange for diplomatic representatives accredited to the Holy See by other governments. The position of Nuncio corresponds to the civil title of ambassador, that of Internucio more or less closely to the civil title of minister.

To the countries which send no diplomatic representatives to the Vatican, the Holy See sends Apostolic Delegates. An Apostolic Delegate is a legate of the Roman Pontiff without diplomatic status.

A. *Apostolic Nuncios and Internuncios*

The Roman Pontiff has the right, independent of any civil authority, to send legates with or without ecclesiastical jurisdic-

---

[38] *ASS*, XXXIX (1906), 535–537.

[39] De Martinis, *Ius Pontificium de Propaganda Fide*, VII (Supplementum et Index), appendix II, 287–316.

[40] *AAS*, XXXII (1940), 235–244. The missionary agreement concluded on May 7, 1940, between the Holy See and Portugal was a part of the general concordat.

[41] *La Documentation Catholique*, II (1919), 195.

tion into every part of the world. This right is the logical corollary of the ordinary and immediate jurisdiction enjoyed by the Roman Pontiff over all members of the Church, inclusive of the hierarchy.[42]

Nuncios and Internuncios are primarily diplomatic representatives of the Holy See accredited directly to the respective governments. They deal with ecclesiastical matters of concern to the Holy See and the civil authority. In addition, they perform duties of a purely ecclesiastical nature which in mission countries will include the unifying, promoting, and supervising of missionary activities.[43]

Through the Secretariat of State, the Roman Pontiff carries on all the diplomatic relations which are necessary in order to insure freedom of action for the Church throughout the world. The designation of all Nuncios and Internuncios pertains to the Secretariat of State, which submits the names of approved candidates to the Roman Pontiff for appointment.[44]

The Apostolic Nuncio in the Philippines, for example, depends upon the Secretariat of State, whose authority extends even to the territories which are subject to the Congregation for the Propagation of the Faith, as well as to territories subject to the Consistorial Congregation.[45] It pertains, however, to the Congregation for the Propagation of the Faith to communicate to the pontifical representatives, Nuncios and Internuncios, the appropriate faculties and instructions for the territories of its competence.[46]

[42] Abbo-Hannan, *The Sacred Canons* (2 vols., St. Louis, London: Herder, 1957), I, 321; can. 265.

[43] *Guida,* p. 49.

[44] M. Martin, "The Secretariat of State," *The Ecclesiastical Review,* XLII (1910), 542.

[45] *Guide des Missions Catholiques,* publié sous le haut patronage de la Sacree Congregation de la Propaganda (Paris, 1937), p. 61. Cf. S.C. pro Negot. Eccl. Extraord., decr. 30 ian. and 30 oct. 1923—*AAS,* XV (1923), pp. 179, 561.

[46] *Loc. cit.*

B. *Apostolic Delegates in the Missions*

The Apostolic Delegates have no diplomatic standing,[47] but they exercise ordinary power in the supervision of religious activities within the territory committed to them, with the obligation of informing the Holy See.[48] Moreover, they receive delegated faculties.[49] They are also the intermediaries between the Holy See and the ordinaries in mission areas, when there is a question of creating or dismembering ecclesiastical territories and of appointing bishops. They supervise the application of general directives given by the Holy See, especially decrees and instructions. Moreover, they promote all the efforts which may expedite the establishment of native Churches.[50]

The following is a list of the Apostolic Delegates.

(1) Consistorial Congregation: Today there are four Apostolic Delegates dependent upon the Consistorial Congregation, that is, for Canada, England, Mexico, and the United States.[51]

(2) Congregation for the Oriental Church: There are six Apostolic Delegates who depend upon the Congregation for the Oriental Church, for Arabia, Bulgaria, Israel, Greece, Iraq, and Turkey.[52]

(3) Congregation for the Propagation of the Faith: Today there are nine Apostolic Delegates dependent upon the Congregation for the Propagation of the Faith. They are located in French Africa, South Africa, East Africa, Albania, Australia, Belgian Congo, Indochina, Korea, and Thailand.[53]

---

[47] Can. 269, §2; Secr. Status, *notificatio*, 8 maii 1916—*AAS*, VIII (1916), 213.

[48] Can. 267, § 1, n. 2.

[49] *Loc. cit.* Cf. can. 267, § 2; Vermeersch, *Periodica de Re Canonica et Morali*, XII (1924), 69-98, 129-159.

[50] Bartocetti, *L'elemento giuridico nel problema del cléro indigeno* (Isola de Liri, 1937), p. 17.

[51] *Annuario Pontifico* for 1960, pp. 987-988.

[52] *Ibid.*, pp. 988-989.

[53] *Ibid.*, pp. 989-990.

ARTICLE 3. PONTIFICAL COMMISSION FOR RUSSIA

On June 20, 1925, the Pontifical Commission for Russia was established, as a section of the Congregation for the Oriental Church, for ecclesiastical matters affecting Russians living in or outside of Russia.[54] Five years later, on April 6, 1930, the Pontifical Commission for Russia was separated by the *motu proprio Inde ab initio* of Pius XI from the Congregation for the Oriental Church. With jurisdiction over all the ecclesiastical affairs of Russia conferred upon it, this Commission was made *sui iuris.*[55] Then, in the *motu proprio Quam sollicita* of December 21, 1934, Pius XI decreed that only matters pertaining to Russian living in Russia were to be entrusted henceforth to the Commission for Russia, and this without prejudice to the rights of the Congregation for the Oriental Church.[56] This means that jurisdiction over the clergy and faithful of the Oriental rites, whether in or outside Russia, was again committed to the Congregation for the Oriental Church.[57]

This Commission was attached to the Congregation for Extraordinary Ecclesiastical Affairs. The affairs and causes of Russians of the Latin rite living in Russia are reserved to the special Commission for Russia; the Russian faithful of the Latin rite living outside of Russia are subjects of the ordinary of the place where they are. The Russians who belong to the Oriental rite, whether they be in or outside of Russia, depend on the Congregation for the Oriental Church.[58]

[54] S.C. Orient. *communicato,* 20 iun. 1926—*AAS,* XVIII (1926), 62; cf. Comm. for Russia, decr. 13 iul. 1928—*AAS,* XX (1928), 260.

[55] Pius XI, motu propr. *Inde ab initio,* 6 apr. 1930—*AAS,* XXII (1930), 153; Bouscaren, *Digest,* I, 259.

[56] Pius XI, motu propr. *Quam sollicita,* 21 dec. 1934—*AAS,* XXVII (1935), 65-66; canon 257.

[57] Staffa, "De Sacrae Congregationis pro Ecclesia Orientali Competentia," *Apollinaris,* XI (1938), 366.

[58] Staffa, *loc. cit.; AAS,* XXVII (1935), 65-66.

CONCLUSIONS

1. The constitution *Inscrutabili,* of June 22, 1622, did not attach any definite limit to the jurisdiction of the Congregation for the Propagation of the Faith on any species of mission affairs. Only matters called *graviora* were to be remitted to the pope. However, the Congregation was accustomed (*solet*) to refer specific matters to the appropriate Congregations for a solution. (Cf. pp. 17-24)

2. On June 22, 1622, the Congregation for the Propagation of the Faith was officially established *de jure* as the exclusive central organization for the territories of the missions, but *de facto* this Congregation could not exercise its full authority, faculty, and power. Its exclusive authority developed gradually through the constant *praxis* of the Congregation. (Cf. pp. 25-26)

3. To overcome the difficulties arising from the rights of Royal Patronage and the privileges of regulars, the Congregation departed from the common law, substituting for the ordinary hierarchy the vicars and prefects apostolic. (Cf. pp. 27-30)

4. The Pontifical Works for the Propagation of the Faith, of St. Peter the Apostle for the Native Clergy, and of the Holy Childhood are not a part of the *instituta ecclesiastica,* since they lack the character of foundation, with endowment of goods, permanent form, etc., of which Canon 1490 speaks. Instead, the three pontifical Works are associations of members of the Church and chiefly of lay people. They are, thus, included in the *associationes fidelium.* (Cf. pp. 43-50)

5. The Congregation for the Propagation of the Faith has true legislative power, although it is restricted in its exercise. The true legislative power is applicable only if some great need of the missions requires it. (Cf. pp. 50-54)

6. In the exercise of jurisdiction in mission regions, the Roman Pontiff is not restricted by any territorial limit. His jurisdiction is exercised freely and independently in mission lands. In practice, however, this immediate authority is not exercised so freely

in all mission countries, since account must be taken of the concordats between the Apostolic See and various nations. (Cf. pp. 55-58)

7. Mission territory may be defined as territory of the Latin rite where the ordinary hierarchy is not yet established, or if established, is still subject to the Congregation for the Propagation of the Faith or remains in the status of mission under another Roman Congregations. (Cf. pp. 58-62)

8. A synod held in an apostolic prefecture or a *missio sui iuris* may be treated in the same way as in a vicariate apostolic, although the Code of Canon Law is silent on the matter. According to the analogy of law, this conclusion may be drawn from Canon 304, § 2, which refers to apostolic prefectures, since § 1 of the same canon (concerning the archives of the mission) places vicars and prefects apostolic on the same basis. (Cf. pp. 67-70)

9. The Congregation for the Propagation of the Faith is incompetent in matters pertaining to the faith, matrimonial cases, and general liturgical norms, all of which are reserved to the appropriate Congregations, namely, the Holy Office, Congregation for the Discipline of the Sacraments, and Congregation of Sacred Rites. However, the Congregation for the Propagation of the Faith does in fact give the decennial faculties for certain cases in virtue of power received from the Roman Pontiff. (Cf. pp. 88-96)

10. In principle, the authority of the Congregation for the Propagation of the Faith affects religious only in their capacity as missionaries. Consequently, with regard to papal approval of religious institutes, it is evident from Canon 252, § 5, that the institutes have to apply to the Congregation for Religious for such approbation, even if they are found in mission land subject to the Congregation for the Propagation of the Faith and, outside mission territories, even if their scope is purely missionary. In practice, however, the Congregation for the Propagation of the Faith has actually approved certain missionary congregations since the promulgation of the Code. These religious institutes are subject to the Congregation even as regards internal discipline in spite of Canon 252, § 5. The law, however, is not changed in this

matter. Instead, particular concessions have been tolerated and allowed by the Holy See. (Cf. pp. 96-105)

11. By the action of Pius XI, the Congregation for the Oriental Church has competence over all Latins, clergy and faithful, including the missions and missionaries, within its territories. Thus, the Congregation for the Propagation of the Faith was deprived of competence over the Latin missions in the areas which are considered Oriental. (Cf. pp. 106-112)

APPENDIX I

The text of the following decennial faculties is from *Periodica de Re Morali Canonica Liturgica*, Tom. XLIX (1960-Fasc. III), pp. 341-352:

SACRA CONGREGATIO DE PROPAGANDA FIDE

Prot. N. 2150/60

FORMULA FACULTATUM DECENNALIUM

Vi potestatis sibi a SS.mo D.N. Joanne Div. Prov. Pp. XXIII tributae, haec S. Congregatio Ordinario
. . . .
sequentes facultates concedit ad decennium, quod decurrit a die 1 mensis Januarii anni 1961 ad diem 31 mensis Decembris anni 1970.

A) Circa Sacramenta Et Sacros Ritus

1. Concedendi sacerdotibus atque diaconis facultatem benedicendi aquam baptismalem per formulam breviorem in Rituali Romano contentam.

2. Conficiendi, si sit Episcopus consecratus, olea sacra cum numero ministrorum quos haberi contigerit; et, si necessitas urgeat, etiam extra diem Coenae Domini.

3. Concedendi sacerdotibus facultatem conficiendi oleum infirmorum, in casu tamen verae necessitatis, id est, si oleum infirmorum, ab Episcopo benedictum, haberi nequeat.

4. Concedendi facultatem administrandi Confirmationis Sacramentum nonnullis sacerdotibus, absente tamen aut longinque residente vel impedito quocumque Episcopo, et servato ritu in Rituali Romano contento.[1]

5. Permittendi ut iusta de causa Missa celebrari possit, super altari portatili, sine ministrante, sub dio et in navi, dummodo, debitis cautelis adhibitis, nullum adsit irreverentiae periculum, et locus decens sit, etiamsi altare sit fractum vel sine Reliquiis Sanctorum; atque ut Missa inchoari queat post mediam noctem.

6. Permittendi ut sacerdotes substituere possint altari portatili seu petrae sacrae aliquod linteum ex lino vel cannabe confectum et rite benedictum, in quo conditae sint Sanctorum Reliquiae ab aliquo Ordinario loci recognitae, super quo iidem sacerdotes sacrosanctum Missae sacrificium celebrare

[1] Cfr. Sacra Congregatio de Propaganda Fide, Decretum confirmatione administranda iis, qui in periculo mortis sunt constituti, A.A.S. 40 (1948), p. 41.

queant iis tantum in casibus in quibus nulla ecclesia vel nullum oratorium publicum exstet, servatis de cetero servandis iuxta Rubricas, praesertim quoad tobaleas et corporale.

7. Permittendi ut Missa celebrari possit cum uno lumine cuiusvis generis; nec non permittendi ut Missa absque luminibus celebrari possit, in casu verae necessitatis.

8. Permittendi ut in utraque purificatione calicis aqua tantum adhiberi possit, dummodo tamen adsit vini penuria.

9. Permittendi thurificationem in Missis a solo celebrante cantatis vel etiam in Missis lectis cum cantu.

10. Concedendi ut Missa solemnis et aliae functiones liturgicae solemnes celebrari possint cum assistentia solius diaconi, si alii ministri sacri desint.

11. Permittendi ut adhibeantur paramenta, vestes sacrae et mappae altaris, confecta ex gossypio vel, exclusis corporalibus, pallis et purificatoriis, ex alia materia, quae deceat.

12. Concedendi sacerdotibus ut, iusta de causa, in celebrando Sancto Sacrificio, uti possint paramentis cuiusvis coloris liturgici.

13. Concedendi sacerdotibus ut bis vel ter in die Missam celebrare possint, si, iuxta prudens Ordinarii iudicium, notabilis partis fidelium bonum id postulet, servatis de caetero iure servandis.

14. Permittendi ut in ecclesiis et oratoriis publicis, quae privilegio iuris communis (can. 821 §§ 2-3) non gaudeant, vel in locis ubi Missa pro fidelibus celebrari soleat, tres Missae statim post mediam noctem Nativitatis Domini celebrari possint, cauto tamen ut omnia cum omni reverentia fiant.

15. Permittendi ut functiones Hebdomadae santae, etiam bis, et ritu simplici, celebrari queant hora postmeridiana, prudenti Ordinarii iudicio statuta, in locis quoque ubi Missa pro fidelibus celebrari solet; et quatenus neque praedictae functiones fieri possint, permittendi ut in iisdem locis Missa lecta Feria Quinta in Coena Domini opportuniori hora litari possit.

16. Permittendi ut in ecclesiis ter infra hebdomadam, extra Quadragesimam, Missa lecta de Requie celebrari possit, etiam diebus ritus duplicis maioris et minoris, exceptis dominicis, octavis Nativitatis Domini, Paschatis et Pentecostes nec non feriis ac vigiliis privilegiatis, diebus tamen, quibus eadem Missae a rubricis permittitur, computatis.

17. Concedendi ut toto anni tempore Missa de Dominica celebrari possit diebus infra Hebdomadam modo ne occurrat festum ritus duplicis primae classis.

18. Permittendi, etiam diebus festis et dominicis, Missam votivam de B.M.V., diebus autem ferialibus etiam Missam defunctorum, iis qui, ob defectum oculorum aliamve infirmitatem, legere nequeant vel nonnisi extremo cum labore Missas singulis diebus occurentes iuxta Missalis Romani rubricas legere valeant.

19. Permittendi ut, iusta de causa, Sanctissimum Sacramentum cum duobus luminibus cuiusvis generis exponi possit. Quoad vero lumina in expositione perpetua et Quadraginta Horarum opportunas Ordinarius loci praescribere potest.

20. Permittendi ut, in locis ubi nulla prorsus materia ad lampades nutriendas haberi potest, Sanctissimum Sacramentum etiam sine lumine asservari possit, onerata conscientia ipsius Ordinarii.

21. Permittendi, si sit periculum irreverentiae vel sacrilegii, ut Sanctissimum Sacramentum in loco non sacro, decenti tamen, retineri possit, etiam sine lumine.

22. Permittendi ut Sanctissima Eucharistia asservari possit ad normam can. 1265, etiamsi sacerdos bis tantum in mense Missam in sacro loco celebret.

23. Permittendi religiosis utriusque sexus ut pallas, corporalia et purificatoria primo abluere valeant (*subdelegabilis*).

24. Permittendi sacerdotibus et diaconis ut, iusta de causa, deferre et administrare valeant christianis aegrotantibus Sanctissimam Eucharistiam sine superpelliceo ac sine comite.

25. Permittendi ut tempus, quo Paschalis communio fieri potest, ad diem Cinerum anticipetur.

26. Conferendi, rationabili de causa, omnes Ordines minores eadem die, etiam cum prima Tonsura.

27. Conferendi, si sit Episcopus, iusta de causa, omnes sacros Ordines etiam Presbyteratum, diebus ferialibus etsi continuis.

28. Permittendi, iusta de causa, ut suis subditis omnes sacri Ordines, etiam Presbyteratus, disbus ferialibus etsi continuis conferri possint.

29. Dispensandi, canonicis existentibus causis, super impedimentis matrimonialibus sive minoris sive maioris gradus (can. 1042), tam publicis quam occultis, etiam multiplicibus, iuris tamen ecclesiastici, exceptis impedimentis provenientibus ex sacro Presbyteratus ordine, ex affinitate in linea recta, consummato matrimonio, et ex defectu praescriptae aetatis, quando sponsi ad aetatem ab antiquo iure praefixam nondum pervenerint (idest ad annum 14 completum pro viris et ad 12 completum pro mulieribus).

Concedendo tamen has dispensationes, Ordinarius prae oculis habeat regulas statutas in Codice, a can. 1035 ad can. 1080, circa impedimenta in genere et in specie et, in impedimentis mixtae religionis et disparitatis cultus, servatis conditionibus ab Ecclesia praescriptis: videlicet de amovendo a catholico coniuge perversionis periculo, ac de universa prole utriusque sexus in catholicae religionis sanctitate tantum baptizanda et educanda,[2] monita parte catholica de obligatione, qua tenetur, conversionem coniugis acatholici prudenter curandi: eaque lege ut, neque ante neque post matrimonium coram Ecclesia initum, partes adeant ministrum falsi cultus ad matrimonialem consensum praestandum vel renovandum. Si agatur vero de matrimoniis cum hebraeis vel mahumetanis, peculiari ratione oportet ut: constet de status libertate partis infidelis, ad removendum periculum polygamiae; absit periculum circumcisionis prolis; et si civilis actus sit ineundus, sit tantum caeremonia civilis nullaque Mahumetis invocatio aut aliud superstitionis genus interveniat (*subdelegabilis*).

[2] Cf. Sylloge ad usum missionariorum, Romae, 1939, p. 561 et ss.

30. Sanandi in radice, iuxta regulas in Codice a can. 1138 ad can. 1141 statutas, matrimonia ob aliquod impedimentum, de quo supra (n. 29) vel ob defectum formae, nulliter contracta. Quoad vero attinet ad prolis legitimationem, Ordinarius prae oculis habeat canones 1051, 1138.

Facultas sanandi in radice non extenditur ad casus in quibus supervenerit amentia unius vel utriusque partis. In singulis hisce casibus igitur ad S. Sedem recurrendum erit (*subdelegabilis*).

31. Sanandi pariter in radice matrimonia mixta attentata coram magistratu civili vel ministro acatholico, dummodo moraliter certum sit partem acatholicam universae prolis nasciturae catholicam educationem non esse impedituram (*subdelegabilis*).

32. Dispensandi super interpellatione coniugum in infidelitate relictorum[3] pro omnibus casibus ordinariis, quando scilicet adhibitis antea omnibus diligentiis, etiam per publicas ephemerides, ad reperiendum locum ubi coniux infidelis habitat, iisque in irritum cessis, constet ex processu saltem summario et extraiudicialiter coniugem absentem moneri legitime non posse aut monitum intra tempus in monitione praefixum suam voluntatem non significasse (*subdelegabilis*).

33. Itemque dispensandi super interpellatione coniugis in infidelitate relicti, siquidem certo constiterit ex processu saltem summario et extraiudicialiter interpellationem fieri non posse sine evidenti gravis damni aut coniugi iam ad finem converso (etsi nondum baptizato), aut christianis inferendi periculo (*subdelegabilis*).

34. Permittendi ut, accedente gravi causa, interpellatio coniugis infidelis ante baptismum partis quae ad fidem convertitur fieri possit; nec non, gravi pariter de causa, ab eadem interpellatione, ante baptismum partis quae convertitur, dispensandi, dummodo hoc in casu ex processu saltem summario et extraiudiciali constet interpellationem fieri non posse, vel fore inutilem (*subdelegabilis*).

35. Concedendi, etiam in dioecesibus, sacerdotibus qui, praedicationis cursibus, quibus vulgo nomen est "missiones," ad evangelizandos fideles vel ad aliud exercitium pietatis implendum in longinquas regiones a parochiali sede dissitas pergunt, iisdem Missionibus perdurantibus, licentiam matrimonii celebrationi valide assistendi, firmis sacrorum canonum praescriptionibus tum de iuribus parochi servandis tum de inscriptione in libris paroecialibus facienda (*subdelegabilis*).

36. Impertiendi benedictionem nuptialem extra Missam aut preces recitandi iuxta formulas in Rituali Romano contentas (*subdelegabilis*).

37. Confirmandi Confessarium ordinarium etiam ad quartum et quintum triennium, servatis conditionibus in canone 526 praescriptis.

38. Permittendi, nomine Sanctae Sedis, ut Moniales e clausura maiore exeant pro brevibus egressibus et in casibus enumeratis in Instructione lata a S.C. de Religiosis die 25 martii 1956 (*subdelegabilis*).

[3] Pro dispensandis infidelibus plures uxores habentibus, ut post baptismum quam ex illis maluerint, si etiam ipsa fidelis fiat, retinere possint, nisi prima voluerit converti, cfr. can. 1125.

B) Circa Absolutiones, Benedictiones, Indulgentias et Indulta Varia

39. Absolvendi ab omnibus censuris, sive simpliciter sive speciali modo Romano Pontifici reservatis, iuxta can. 2250 § 3 (*subdelegabilis*).

40. Dispensandi vel commutandi, iusta de causa, vota privata, Sedi Apostolicae reservata, de quibus in can. 1309 (*subdelegabilis*).

41. Benedicendi solo crucis signo cum omnibus Indulgentiis a Sancta Sede concedi solitis, coronas precatorias, cruces, parvas statuas et sacra numismata, et adnectendi coronis Indulgentias, quae a S. Birgitta et quae a Patribus Crucigeris nuncupantur (*subdelegabilis*).

42. Conferendi uni alterive i.e. paucis ex sacerdotibus in casu necessitatis facultatem consecrandi, iuxta formam in Pontificali Romano praescriptam, calices, patenas et, iuxta formulam breviorem, altarium lapides, adhibitis tamen oleis ab Episcopo benedictis.

Pariter conferendi facultatem benedicendi linteum secundum formulam specialem in Rituali Romano contentam.

43. Impertiendi, praeter concessiones communes a Sancta Sede factas, ter in anno in solemnioribus festis Benedictionem Papalem iuxta praescriptam formulam cum Indulgentia plenaria ab iis lucranda, qui vere poenitentes, confessi et Sacra Communione refecti, eidem Benedictioni interfuerint, Deumque pro sanctae Fidei propagatione et iuxta mentem Summi Pontificis oraverint.

44. Concedendi ut, servatis consuetis conditionibus, Indulgentiam plenariam in primae Communionis solemni distributione et in Sacramenti Confirmationis administratione, christifideles omnes praesentes lucrari possint.

45. Concedendi Indulgentiam plenariam primo conversis ab haeresi, servatis consuetis conditionibus (*subdelegabilis*).

46. Concedendi Indulgentiam plenariam singulis ex clero et ex religiosis utriusque sexus, qui per tres saltem integros dies spiritualibus Exercitiis interfuerint, ac sacrosanctum Missae sacrificium celebrantes vel saltem ad Sacram Synaxim accedentes, pias preces fuderint, ut supra (n. 43).

47. Impertiendi Benedictionem Apostolicam cum Indulgentia plenaria omnibus christifidelibus, qui spiritualibus Exercitiis seu sacris Missionibus, de quibus in can. 1349 § 1, ultra medietatem interfuerint, benedictioni cum Cruce in fine postremae concionis impertiendae vere poenitentes, confessi ac Sacra Communione refecti adstiterint, atque ecclesiam, in qua conciones huiusmodi habebuntur devote visitaverint, ibique pias ad Deum preces fuderint, ut supra (n. 43) (*subdelegabilis*).

48. Concedendi in actu visitationis paroeciarum, quasi-paroeciarum et missionum, nec non communitatum tam saecularium quam religiosorum, ut Indulgentiam plenariam una vice tantum lucrari possint christifideles, dummodo contriti, confessi ac Sacra Communione refecti ecclesiam vel oratorium visitaverint et pias ad Deum preces fuderint, ut supra (n. 43) (*subdelegabilis*).

49. Concedendi christifidelibus ut Indulgentias, propter quas confessio saltem bis in mense requiritur, lucrari possint, etsi semel in mense ad poenitentiae sacramentum accesserint (*subdelegabilis*).

50. Iisdem christifidelibus largiendi, si loca inhabitent ubi prorsus impossibile vel saltem sit difficile ad confessarium accedere, ut lucrari queant Indulgentias, quae Confessionem et Communionem requirunt, dummodo sint corde saltem contriti, addito firmo proposito peccata, quamprimum poterunt, confidendi (*subdelegabilis*).

51. Benedicendi Christi crucifixi imagines sculptas cum Indulgentia plenaria a quocumque ex fidelibus in mortis periculo constitutis lucranda eas deosculando, vel Sanctissimum Iesu nomen corde saltem, si ore non potuerint, invocando (*subdelegabilis*).

52. Erigendi, vel concedendi sacerdotibus facultatem erigendi, ritibus ab Ecclesia praescriptis, stationes Viae crucis, cum omnibus indulgentiis, quae huiusmodi pium exercitium peragentibus a Summis Pontificibus impertitae sunt; et applicandi easdem indulgentias crucibus et crucifixis, pro infirmis aliisque legitime impeditis, dummodo iidem crucifixum ad hoc benedictum cum affectu et animo contrito osculentur vel etiam tantum intueantur, brevem insimul, si possint, aliquam orationem vel precem iaculatoriam in memoriam Passionis et Mortis Domini recitantes.

53. Erigendi illas etiam confraternitates a Sancta Sede adprobatas quarum instituendarum ius apostolico ex privilegio aliis reservatum est (can. 686 § 2) (una excepta confraternitate Sacratissimi Rosarii) iisque adscribendi christifideles.

54. Concedendi sacerdotibus facultatem christifideles adscribendi confraternitatibus (inclusa confraternitate Sacratissimi Rosarii) atque benedicendi, ritibus ab Ecclesia praescriptis, omnia scapularia a Sede Apostolica probata, eaque imponendi sine onere inscriptionis.

55. Concedendi ut privatim recitari possit matutinum cum laudibus diei sequentis statim post meridiem.

56. Concedendi sacerdotibus diaconis et subdiaconis ut ob legitimum gravemque rationem, loco Divini Officii, Rosarium integrum aut alias preces recitare possint.

57. Permittendi clericis ut vestes laicales induere possint, si aliter vel transire ad loca eorum curae commissa, vel in eis commode permanere nequeant.

58. Permittendi clericis et religiosis ut ad finem Regni Christi amplius dilatandi, medicinam et chirurgiam exercere valeant dummodo in istis artibus revera periti sint et in curandis infirmis omnia quae clericum et religiosum dedecent, vel scandalo esse possint, diligenter vitent, atque pro ipso exercitio artis suae nihil accipiant.

59. Dispensandi cum catholicis ut serviliter laborare valeant diebus Dominicis, vel festis de praecepto, exceptis Paschate et Pentecoste, post tamen Sanctae Missae auditionem, si possit audiri; si vero non possit, recitatis precibus suppletivis (*subdelegabilis*).

60. Permittendi ut, servatis rubricis, in dominicam proxime sequentem

transferatur solemnitas festorum, quae secundum can. 1247 sunt ferianda, sed legitime abolita.

61. Transferendi processiones Rogationum in dies, quae secundum adiuncta locorum aptiores Ordinario videantur.

62. Concedendi, non ultra triennium, licentiam legendi ac retinendi, sub custodia tamen ne ad aliorum manus perveniant libros prohibitos et ephemerides, exceptis operibus haeresim vel schisma ex professo pro pugnantibus, vel etiam ipsa religionis fundamenta evertere nitentibus necnon operibus de obscoenis ex professo tractantibus, singulis christifidelibus sibi subditis, nonnisi tamen cum delectu ac rationabili de causa (cfr. can. 1042 § 2), iis scilicet tantum, qui eorundem librorum et ephemeridum lectione sive ad ea impugnanda sive ad proprium legitimum munus exercendum, vel iustum studiorum curriculum peragendum, vere indigeant.

C) Pro Ipso Ordinario
(excepto Vicario Generali et Delegato)

63. Asservandi in sacello domus stabilis suae residentiae actualis Sanctissimum Eucharistiae Sacramentum atque etiam pro Ordinario, charactere episcopali carente, fruendi indulto personali altaris privilegiati quotidiani.

64. Lucrandi indulgentias, quas aliis vi facultatum sibi concessarum impertire valet, impletis tamen consuetis conditionibus.

65. Si sit Episcopus, utendi throno cum baldachino et cappa magna in Pontificalibus; nec non permittendi presbyteris, in ecclesiis suae iurisdictionis celebrantibus, ut sui nominis tamquam Antistitis sive in precibus ferialibus sive in Canone Missae mentio fiat: quatenus haec a iure concessa non fuerint.

66. Pro Praefectis Apostolicis, utendi, durante munere, insignibus et privilegiis, ipsis a can. 308 concessis, etiam extra proprium territorium, praehabito, quoad exercitium Pontificalium, consensu Ordinarii.

67. Vestiendi paramentis pontificalibus, rationabili de causa, sine rocheto, tunicella et dalmatica.

68. Celebrandi, quando ob penuriam sacerdotum impossibilis sit Missae pontificalis litatio, Missam solemnem aut Missam in cantu sicut ceteri sacerdotes.

Animadversiones

I. Memoratae facultates ea lege conceduntur, ut illae tantum subdelegari possint, quae ita explicite notantur per verbum *"subdelegabilis."*

II. Ordinarius, inclusis Vicario Generali et Delegato, uti potest, in iisdem tamen adiunctis, facultatibus seu permissionibus, quas, intra limites in praecedentibus articulis expressos, concedere potest.

III. Ordinarius insuper supradicitis omnibus facultatibus sive per se sive per alios uti tantum valeat intra fines suae iurisdictionis; easque gratis et sine ulla mercede exerceat (praeterquam pro expensis Cancellariae et cursus postalis ab iis qui pares sunt ad eas solvendas exigendis) et facta mentione apostolicae delegationis (vel subdelegationis ab Ordinario).

IV. Quod si forte ex oblivione vel inadvertentia ultra tempus supra praefinitum, hisce facultatibus Ordinarium, vel eius delegatum, uti contingat, absolutiones, dispensationes, concessiones omnes exinde impertitae uti ratae atque validae habeantur. Insuper datis ab Ordinario precibus pro renovatione seu prorogatione earundem facultatum, ipsae in suo robore perseverare censeantur, usque dum responsum S.C. ad eundem Ordinarium pervenerit.

Datum Romae, ex Aedibus Sacrae Congregationis de Propaganda Fide, die ... mensis .... anno Domini .....

. . . .

. . . .

NB.—Cetera rescripta concessa usque ad expirationem facultatum generalium debent remitti ad S.C. de Propaganda Fide pro renovatione. Gratis sine ulla solutione quocumque titulo.

APPENDIX II

Chronological list of documents pertinent to the missions, taken from *Acta Apostolicae Sedis* from 1909 to 1960:

1. S.C. Off., "Conceduntur indulgentiae recitantibus orationem pro conversione imperii Sinensis et Mongoliae," 27 maii 1909—*AAS*, I (1909), 513-514.
2. S.C. Off., "Indulgentia conceditur recitantibus quamdam orationem pro conversione Imperii Iaponensis," 8 iul. 1909—*AAS*, I (1909), 576.
3. Pius X, litt. encycl. *Lacrimabili statu*, "Litterae Encyclicae ad archiepiscopos et episcopos Americae Latinae de misera Indorum conditione sublevanda," 7 iun. 1912—*AAS*, IV (1912), 521-525.
4. S. Poenit Ap., "Amplificatur indulgentia iam concessa recitantibus orationem pro conversione Iaponiae," 28 febr. 1919—*AAS*, XI (1919), 153.
5. Secr. Status, ep. *Inter multiplices*, "Epistola ad R.D. sac. Rogerium de Teil, Societatis a Sancta Infantia moderatorem: missis quinquaginta francorum millibus, piam sodalitatem vehementer B.P. adhortatur ut, pro augentibus missionum necessitatibus, fusiore in posterum manu, ad ecclesiasticam indigenarum institutionem conferat," 28 maii 1919—*AAS*, XI (1919), 249-250.
6. Benedictus XV, allocutio, 3 iul. 1919—*AAS*, XI (1919), 259 (De missionibus).
7. Benedictus XV, ep. ap. *Maximum illud*, "Encyclica de fide catholica per orbem terrarum propaganda," 30 nov. 1919—*AAS*, XI (1919), 440-455.
8. S.C.P.F., ep. *Summus Pontifex*, "Epistola ad universos sacrorum antistites de stipe colligenda pro nigritis in Africa," 29 sept. 1919—*AAS*, XII (1920), 74-75.
9. S.C.P.F., decr. *Ut missionum*, "Decretum super adprobatione operis S. Petri Apostoli," 26 apr. 1920—*AAS*, XII (1920), 247.
10. S.C.P.F., instr. *Cum a pluribus*, "Instructio circa erectionem quasiparoeciarum in vicariatibus et praefecturis apostolics," 25 iul. 1920—*AAS*, XII (1920), 331-333.
11. Secr. Status, ep. "Epistola ad Card. Van Rossum, S.C. de Prop. Fide Praefectum, circa pontificium opus a S. Petro Apostolo pro clero indigena in sacris missionibus efformando," 10 aug. 1920—*AAS*, XII (1920), 345-346.
12. Benedictus XV, allocutio, 16 dec. 1920—*AAS*, XII (1920), 588 (De missionibus).

13. S.C.P.F., decr. *Ordinarii*, Decretum de definiendis limitibus paroeciarum in dioecesibus S. Cong. de Prop. Fide subiectis," 9 dec. 1921—*AAS*, XIII (1921), 17-18.

14. S.C.P.F., litt. *Gloriosissime*, "Litterae circulares ad universos locorum ordinarios tertis exeunte saeculo ab instituta Sacra Congregatione," 3 dec. 1921—*AAS*, XIII (1921), 561-562.

15. Benedictus XV, *O. Gesù*, 17 nov. 1921—*AAS*, XIII (1921), 564 (Preghiera per la propagazione della Fide).

16. Benedictus XV, ep. *Libenter quidem*, "Epistola ad Delegatum Apostolicum in Indiis Orientalibus: nonnulla paterne admonens in ecclesiae utilitatem," 15 oct. 1921—*AAS*, XIV (1922), 7-10.

17. S.C.R., "Rescripta: de additione opportunae invocationis Litaniis Sanctorum et de celebratione Missae votivae pro Fidei propagatione semel in anno in qualibet dioecesi," 22 mart. 1922—*AAS*, XIV (1922), 200-201.

18. S.C.P.F., ep. *Sacrum consilium*, "Epistola ad episcopos, vicarios, praefectosque apostolicos ac missionum superiores: de relationibus missionum, singulis quinquenniis exhibendis," 16 apr. 1922—*AAS*, XIV (1922), 287-302.

19. Pius XI, motu propr. *Romanorum Pontificum*, "De pio opere a propagatione fidei amplificando," 3 maii 1922—*AAS*, XIV (1922), 321-330.

20. Pius XI, homilia, *Accipietibus virtutem*, "Homilia de Fidei propagatione; habita inter Missarum solemnia, sacra Pentecostes die, in Templo Vaticano," die Pentecostes, 1922—*AAS*, XIV (1922), 344-348.

21. Pius XI, ep. *Fidei propagandae*, "Epistola ad Card. Van Rossum, S. Cong. de Prop. Fide Praefectum: de expositione missionaria in Urbe Anno Sancto MDCCCCXXV habenda," 24 apr. 1923—*AAS*, XV (1923), 222-223.

22. Pius XI, allocutio, 23 maii 1923—*AAS*, XV (1923), 247-248 (De missionibus).

23. S.C.P.F., decr. "Ad superiores ordinum et congregationum religiosarum, quae sacris missionibus provehendis se devovent, nonnulla commendantur ad ipsorum operam uberiorem efficiendam salutarium fructuum," 20 maii 1923—*AAS*, XV (1923), 369-372.

24. S.C.P.F., decr. "Ad omnes ordinarios catholicae ecclesiae: de expositione missionaria in urbe anno iubilari MDCCCXXV instituenda," 3 maii, 1923—*AAS*, XV (1923), 372-373.

25. S.C.P.F., decr. "Ad omnes vicarios, praefectos apostolicos aliosque missionum moderatores: de expositione missionaria," 3 maii 1923—*AAS*, XV (1923), 374-378.

26. Pius XI, allocutio, *Amplissimum*, 24 mart. 1924—*AAS*, XVI (1924), 127-129 (De missionibus).

27. Pius XI, allocutio, *Nostis*, 18 dec. 1924—*AAS*, XVI (1924), 490 (De missionibus).

28. Pius XI, allocutio, *Si frequentia*, 30 mart. 1925—*AAS*, XVII (1925), 122-123 (De missionibus).

29. Pius XI, litt. encycl. *Rerum ecclesiae*, "De sacris missionibus provehendis," 28 febr. 1926—*AAS*, XVIII (1926), 65-83.

30. S.C.P.F., decr. *Ut pia*, "Promulgantur statuta generalia Piae Unionis Cleri pro missionibus atque summarium spiritualium favorum quibus eiusdem Piae Unionis sodales fruuntur," 4 apr. 1926—*AAS*, XVIII (1926), 230-236.

31. S. Poenit. Ap., "Preghiera per le sante missioni indulgentia donata," 18 maii, 1926—*AAS*, XVIII (1926), 322-323.

32. Pius XI, ep. *Ab ipsis*, "Epistola ad vicarios et praefectos apostolicos Sinarum regionibus: adversus quasdam fallaces opiniones de ecclesiae opera in eas gentes," 15 iun. 1926—*AAS*, XVIII (1926), 303-307.

33. Pius XI, "Homilia ad novensiles episcopos e clero indigena Sinensi, habita inter Missarum solemnia consecrationis eorumdum in festo SS. App. Simonis et Iudae, die XXVIII octobris MDCCCCXXVI in Basilica Vaticana," 28 oct. 1926—*AAS*, XVIII (1926), 432-433.

34. Pius XI, motu propr. *Quoniam tam*, "De Museo missionali ethnologico constituendo," 12 nov. 1926—*AAS*, XVIII (1926), 478-479.

35. S.C.R., "Rescriptum de paenultima octobris dominica precibus et actioni pro missionibus peculiariter addicenda," 14 apr. 1926—*AAS*, XVIII (1927), 23-24.

36. Pius XI, allocutio, *Amplissimum*, 20 iun. 1927—*AAS*, XIX (1927), 233-234 (De missionibus).

37. Pius XI, "Homilia habita patriarchali Basilica Vaticana inter solemnia consecrationis episcopi Nagasakiensis die festo Christi Regis," 1927—*AAS*, XIX (1927), 379-380.

38. S.C.R. "Dioecesium et vicariatuum apostolicorum in missionibus: de ipsarum Patrona S. Teresia a Puero Iesu," 14 dec. 1927—*AAS*, XX (1928), 147-148.

39. Pius XI, motu propr. *Decessor noster*, "De pontificorum operum missionalium coordinatione," 24 iun. 1929—*AAS*, XXI (1929), 342-345.

40. Pius XI, motu propr. *Vix ad Summi Pontificatus*, "Pontificum opus a S. Petro apostolo pro cleri indigenae institutione propriis et definitis statutis donatur," 24 iun. 1929—*AAS*, XXI (1929), 345-349.

41. S.C.P.F., instr. *Quum huic*, "Instructio ad vicarios praefectosque apostolicos et ad superiores institutorum, quibus a S. Sede missiones concreditae sunt," 8 dec. 1929—*AAS*, XXII (1930), 111-115.

42. Pius XI, *Qui arcano Dei*, "Nuncium radiophonicum ad universam creaturam," 12 febr. 1931—*AAS*, XXIII (1931), 65-70.

43. Pius XI, allocutio, *Iterum vos*, 13 mart. 1933—*AAS*, XXV (1933), 107-108. (De missionibus).

44. S. Poenit, Ap., decr. *Appropinquante*, "Indulgentiis augetur dies pro missionibus," 1 aug. 1934—*AAS*, XXVI (1934), 526-527.

45. S.C.P.F., instr. *Constans*, "Instructio pro religiosis mulierum institutis,

ad tuendam puerorum matrumque vitam in locis missionum," 11 febr. 1936—*AAS*, XXVIII (1936), 208-209.

46. S. Poenit. Ap., decr. *Summus*, "Indulgentiae extenduntur pio exercitio quod dies pro missionibus nuncupatur," 25 mart. 1936—*AAS*, XXVIII (1936), 308.

47. S.C.P.F., instr. *Pluries*, "Instructio ad Delegatum Apostolicum in Iaponia, circa catholicorum officia erga patriam," 26 maii 1936—*AAS*, XXVIII (1936), 406-409.

48. Pius XI, *Quamquam vobis*, "Nuntius radiophonicus ad urbem Manilam datus ad exitum Congressus Unversalis XXXIII Eucharistici," 23 febr. 1937—*AAS*, XXIX (1937), 17-18.

49. S.C.P.F., instr. *In terris missionum*, "Instructio de congregationibus indigenis condendis," 19 mart. 1927—*AAS*, XXIX (1937), 275-278.

50. Pius XI, ep. ap. *Missionalium rerum*, "Epistola apostolica ad Card. Fumasoni Biondi: quae in missionum regionibus et in orientalis ritus ecclesiastica colitur expositione, in Vaticano a.d. MDCCCCXL habenda," 14 Sept. 1937—*AAS*, XXIX (1937), 413-415.

51. S.C.P.F., decr. *Piae unionis cleri*, "Statuta generalia Piae Unionis Cleri pro missionibus, revisa ac recognita, approbantur," 14 apr. 1937 —*AAS*, XXIX (1937), 435-441.

52. S.C.P.F., instr. *Non semel*, "Instructio circa prudentiorem de rebus missionalibus tractandi rationem," 9 iun. 1939—*AAS*, XXXI (1939), 269-270.

53. Pius XII, "Homilia in Basilica Vaticana habita, inter sacra solemnia, quibus XII episcopos ad missiones regendas destinatos consecravit," 29 oct. 1939—*AAS*, XXXI (1939), 595-598.

54. S.C.P.F., instr. *Plane*, "Instructio circa quasdam caeremonias et iuramentum super ritibus sinensibus," 8 dec. 1939—*AAS*, XXXII (1940), 24-26.

55. Pius XII, ep. encycl. *Saeculo exeunte octavo*, "Epistola encyclica ad hierarchiam Lusitaniae: apostolica missionalium opera enixe Lusitanis commendantur," 13 iun. 1940—*AAS*, XXXII (1940), 249-260.

56. Pius XII, "Nuntius radiophonicus ordinariis et christifidelibus foederatorum Americae septentrionalis civitatum datus, in pervigilio diei pro missionibus," 19 oct. 1940—*AAS*, XXXII (1940), 424-427.

57. S.C.P.F., instr. *Antequam*, "Instructio de novis praefecturis aut vicariatibus apostolicis aut dioecesibus condendis," 21 iun. 1942—*AAS*, XXXIV (1942), 347-349.

58. Pius XII, allocutio, *Vivamento gradito*, "Allocutio habita praesulibus ac officialibus pontificiarum operum missionalium Romae coadunatis," 24 iun. 1944—*AAS*, XXXV (1944), 207-211.

59. Pius XII, const. ap. *Quoties nos*, "Hierarchia episcopalis in Sinis instituitur," 11 apr. 1946—*AAS*, XXXVIII (1946), 301-313.

60. Pius XII, ep. *En prenant connaissance*, "Epistola ad Excmum Tokiensem archiepiscopum ceterosque Iaponiae episcopos," 17 maii 1946—*AAS*, XXXVIII (1946), 345-346.

61. S.C.P.F., decr. *Quo aptius,* "Pro missionibus Coreae Visitator Apostolicus nominatur," 17 iul. 1947—*AAS,* XXXIX (1947), 463.

62. S.C.P.F., decr. *Opus apostolicum,* "De consilio generali operis apostolici in Hibernia constituendo," 18 nov. 1947—*AAS,* XXXX (1948), 423-425.

63. Pius XII, litt. ap. *A missionibus,* "Delegatio Apostolica pro Corea erigitur," 7 apr. 1949—*AAS,* XXXXII (1950), 327.

64. Pius XII, ep. *Perlibenti quidem,* "Ad Eṁum P.D. Petrum tit. S. Crucis in Hierusalem S.R.E. Presb. Cardinalem Fumasoni Biondi, S. Congregationis de Propaganda Fide Praefectum, ob conventum de gationis missionis approbantur," 19 iul. 1953—*AAS,* XXXXVII (1950), 725-728.

65. Pius XII, litt. encycl. *Evangelii praecones,* "De sacris missionibus provehendis," 11 iun. 1951—*AAS,* XXXXIII (1951), 497-528.

66. Pius XII, ep. *Praeses consilii,* "Ad Eṁum P.D. Petrum tit. S. Crucis in Hierusalem S.R.E. Presb. Cardinalem Fumasoni Biondi, Sacri Consilii Catholicae Propagandae Fidei Praefectum: de assignanda die singulis annis ad opus pontificum a Sancta Infantia precibus ac collate stipe promovendum," 4 dec. 1950—*AAS,* XXXXIII (1951), 88-89.

67. Pius XII, allocutio, *Les commémorations,* "Ad moderatores et cooperatores missionalium operum: de fovendo apostolatu pro missionibus," 28 apr. 1952—*AAS,* XXXXIV (1952), 425-429.

68. S.C.P.F., instr. *Plurimis abhinc annis,* "De apto modo pro missionibus stipem corrogandi," 29 iun. 1952—*AAS,* XXXXIV (1952), 549-551.

69. Pius XII, nuntius, "Ob diem pro missionibus datus," 18 oct. 1953—*AAS,* XXXXV (1953), 691-695.

70. Pius XII, ep. ap. *Carissimis Russiae populis,* "Ad universos Russiae populos," 7 iul. 1952—*AAS,* XXXXIV (1952), 505-511.

71. Pius XII, litt. ap. *Evangelium ad pauperes,* "Constitutiones congregationis missionis approbantur," 19 iul. 1953—*AAS,* XXXXVII (1955), 141-142.

72. Pius XII, allocutio, "Iis qui interfuerunt conventui internationali moderatorum sodalitatis ab apostolatu orationis," 27 sept. 1956—*AAS,* XXXXVIII (1956), 674-677.

73. Pius XII, litt. encycl. *Fidei donum,* "De catholicarum missionum condicionibus praesertim in Africa," 21 apr. 1957—*AAS,* XXXXIX (1957), 225-248.

74. S. Poenit. Ap., *O Gesù,* "Oratio pro sacris missionibus ad populum, a Summo Pontifice Pio XII exarata et indulgentiis ditata," 21 maii 1958—*AAS,* L (1958), 490-491.

75. S.C.R., decr., gen. *Novum rubricum,* 26 iul. 1960—*AAS,* LII (1960), 659.

APPENDIX III

The Congregation for the Propagation of the Faith—1960

The following are the members and officials of the Congregation as listed in the *Annuario Pontificio* for 1960:

Cardinals

Gregorio Pietro XV Agagianian, Prefect
Eugenio Tisserant, Bishop of Porto and Santa Rufina
Clemente Micara, Bishop of Velletri
Benedetto Aloisi Masella, Bishop of Palestrina
Marcello Mimmi, Bishop of Sabina and Poggio Mirteto

Joseph Ernest van Roey	Paolo Giobbe
Cerejeira Manuel Gonçalves	Giuseppe Fietta
Ignace Gabriel Tappouni	Amleto Giovanni Cicognani
Pierre Gerlier	Carlo Confalonieri
James Charles McGuigan	Richard James Cushing
Thomas Norman Gilroy	Paul Marie A. Richaud
Francis Spellman	Domenico Tardini
Teodosio Clemente de Gouveia	Albert Gregory Meyer
Thomas Tien Ken-sin	Nicola Canali
Pietro Ciriaci	Alfredo Ottaviani
James Francis McIntyre	Alberto Di Jorio
Valerian Gracias	Francesco Roberti

Most Rev. Pietro Sigismondi, Titular Archbishop of Neapoli in Pisidia,
Secretary
Msgr. Carlo Corvo, Subsecretary
Msgr. Giovanni Antonazzi, Prosecretary of Fiscal Department

Consultors
(The asterisk indicates that the Consultor lives outside of Rome)

Most Rev. Giuseppe Nunes de Costa, Patriarch and Archbishop of Odesso
Most Rev. Pietro Pisani, Titular Archbishop of Costanza in Sycizia
Most Rev. *David Mathew, Titular Archbishop of Apamea in Bitinia
Most Rev. Pietro Parente, Titular Archbishop of Tolemaide in Tebaide
Most Rev. Giovanni Smit, Titular Bishop of Paralo
Most Rev. *Giuseppe Pietro Gagnor, O.P., Bishop of Alessandria
Most Rev. *Martino Lucas, S.V.D., Titular Archbishop of Aduli
Most Rev. Tarcisio E.G., van Valenberg, O.F.M. Cap., Titular Bishop of
Comba
Most Rev. Vittorio Bartoccetti

Msgr. Decio Botti
Msgr. Antonio Piolanti
Msgr. Giuseppe Monticone
Msgr. Garofalo Salvatore

Very Rev. *Crisostomo Schmid, O.S.B., Archabbot
Very Rev. *Edoardo Schröder, S.J.
Very Rev. Francesco Ferraironi, O.M.D.
Very Rev. Callisto Lopinot, O.F.M. Cap.
Very Rev. *Augusto Brault, M.Sp.S.
Very Rev. Timoteo Bouscaren, S.J.

Very Rev. Michele Schulien, S.V.D.
Very Rev. Alberto Perbal, O.M.I.
Very Rev. Petro Rutten, O.S.Cr.
Very Rev. Di Gesù e Maria Vittore, O.C.D.
Very Rev. Francesco Rosenbaum, S.V.D.
Very Rev. Fredegando Callaey, O.F.M.Cap.

Very Rev. Vincenzo A. McCormick, S.J.
Very Rev. Paolo Dezza, S.J.
Very Rev. Ludovico Buijs, S.J.
Very Rev. Bonaventura Mariani, O.F.M.
Very Rev. Da Mondreganes Pio, O.F.M.Cap.
Very Rev. Amando Reuter, O.M.I.

Very Rev. Andreas Seumois, O.M.I.

Minutanti

Msgr. Adamo Pucci
Msgr. Saverio Paventi
Msgr. Pompeo Borgna
Msgr. Edoardo Pecoraio

Msgr. Mariano Clementi
Msgr. Tiziano Scalzotto
Msgr. Giovanni Belej
Very Rev. Giovanni Manning, M.M.

Archivist

Very Rev. Nicola Kowalsky, O.M.I., Archivist General
Very Rev. Agostino Biocchi, O.S.B., Assistant To Archivist General
Msgr. Lujo Schorer, Official of the Office of Statistics

Protocolist and Mailing

Msgr. Francesco Mocchiutti
Msgr. Mario Cipriani
Rev. Vincenzo D. Pediconi

Clerks

Sig. Pietro Micca
Very Rev. Roberto Watteyne, S.M.A.
Sig. Tarcisio Cimetta

Library

Very Rev. Giovanni Rommerskirchen, O.M.I., Librarian
Sig. Pietro Dott Ciatti, Assistant Librarian
Sig. Tullio Ficola, Secretary

THE ADDRESS OF THE CONGREGATION

Petitions to the Congregation for the Propagation of the Faith should be addressed *Beatissime Pater*, as in the case of the other Congregations, but should be sent to the Prefect of the Congregation directly:

All'Eminentissimo e Reverendissimo Signor Cardinale Prefetto della S. Congregazione de Propaganda Fide, Pallazo di Propaganda Fide, Piazza di Spagna, Roma.

The address of the Secretary of the Congregation is:
Excellentissimo Sigismondi Pietro, Secretario
Piazza di Spagna 48, Roma

The address of the Subsecretary of the Congregation is:
Reverendissimo Corvo Carlo, Sotto-Secretario
Via dei Corridori, 64, Roma

ADMINISTRATION OF TEMPORALITIES

Section I (Accounting and Cash)

Accounting

Sig. Mario Rag. Cav. Dott Beni, Chief Accountant
Sig. Pietro Rag. Cav. de Strobel, Sub-Chief Accountant
Sig. Vincenzo Rag. Cav. Ottaviani, Accountant
Sig. Francesco Saladino Saladini, Accountant
Sig. Francesco Rag. Di Pasqua, Accountant
Sig. Antonio Dott. Peda, Accountant
Sig. Mario Rag. Perrone, Assistant Accountant
Sig. Franco Rag. Tiradritto, Clerk

Cash

Sig. Mario Dott. Cav. Angeloni, Cashier
Sig. Renzo Dott. Cardoni, Tax Collector

Section II (Secretariat)

Sig. Aldo Avv. Prof. Comm. Merlino, Minutant
Sig. Renzo Avv. Cav. de Bonis, Minutant
Msgr. Luigi Catenelli, Minutant

Section III (Technical and Legal)

Most Rev. Carolo Principe Avv. Cav. di Gr. Cr. Don Pacelli,
Legal Consultor
Most Rev. Giulio Principe Avv. Cav. di Gr. Cr. Don Pacelli,
Legal Procurator
Sig. Clemente Ing. Comm. Busiri, Architect
Sig. Raffaele Dott. Ing. Cav. Orlandi, Agronomist
Sig. Quirino, Geom. Candola, Official of the Technical Service

COMMISSION FOR THE REVISION

of episcopal synods and conferences, and of the constitutions of the religious institutes which depend upon the Congregation for the Propagation of the Faith and also of the regulation of regional native seminaries

Most Rev. Giovanni Smit, Titular Bishop of Paralo, President
Msgr. Paventi Saverio, Secretary
Very Rev. Callisto, Lopinot, O.F.M. Cap., Consultor
Very Rev. Pietro Rutten, O.S.Cr., Consultor
Very Rev. Di Gesu e Maria Vittore, O.C.D., Consultor
Very Rev. Timoteo Bouscaren, S.J., Consultor
Very Rev. Francesco Rosenbaum, S.V.D., Consultor
Very Rev. Ludovico Buijs, S.J., Consultor
Very Rev. Amando Reuter, O.M.I., Consultor

SUPREME DIRECTIVE COMMITTEE FOR THE PONTIFICAL WORKS FOR THE PROPAGATION OF THE FAITH AND ST. PETER THE APOSTLE, AND ALSO OF THE PONTIFICAL MISSIONARY UNION FOR THE CLERGY

Most Rev. Pietro Sigismondi, Titular Archbishop of Neapoli in Pisidia, Secretary of the Congregation for the Propagation of the Faith, President

Consultors

Most Rev. Giovanni Battista, Leone Nigris, Titular Archbishop of Filippi, Secretary General of the Pontifical Society for the Propagation of the Faith

Most Rev. Faustino Tissot, S.X., Bishop of Chengchow (expulsed), Secretary General of the Pontifical Missionary Union for the Clergy

Msgr. Giovanni Battista di Leguigno Scapinelli, Subsecretary of the Congregation for Extraordinary Ecclesiastical Affairs

Msgr. Ernesto Civardi, Substitute of the Consistorial Congregation

Msgr. Amerigo Giovanelli, Substitute of the Congregation for the Oriental Church

Msgr. Antonio Mazza, Secretary General of the Pontifical Association of St. Peter the Apostle

Most Rev. Francesco J. Brennan, from the Pontifical Society for the Propagation of the Faith

Very Rev. Alberto Perbal, O.M.I., from the Pontifical Association of St. Peter the Apostle

GENERAL SUPERIOR COUNCIL OF THE PONTIFICAL WORKS OF THE PONTIFICAL SOCIETY FOR THE PROPAGATION OF THE FAITH

Most Rev. Pietro Sigismondi, Titular Archbishop of Neapoli in Pisidia, Secretary of the Congregation for the Propagation of the Faith, President

Msgr. Andrea Baron, Vice-President

Most Rev. Giovanni Battista, Leone Nigris, Titular Archbishop of Filippi, Secretary General

Msgr. Armando Valori, Vice-Secretary and Accountant

Msgr. Enrico Pitzky, Assistant to the Secretary

Sig. Carolo Cav. Ser-Marini, Cashier

Consultors

The presidents of the central or national council of the works and the following residents in Rome who belong to various nationalities.

Most Rev. Faustino Tissort, S.X., Bishop of Chengchow, in China (expulsed), from the International Secretary of the Pontifical Missionary Union for the Clergy

Msgr. Amerigo Giovanelli, from the Congregation for the Oriental Church

Msgr. Antonio Mazza, from the Pontifical Association of St. Peter the Apostle

Very Rev. Uberto D. Noots, O. Praem, Abbot General, from Belgium

Msgr. Silvio Beltrami, from Italy

Msgr. Romualdo Bissonnette, from Canada

Most Rev. Francesco J. Brennan, from U.S.A.

Msgr. Guglielmo Clapperton, from Scotland

Msgr. Leonardo Giuseppe Guglielmo Damen, from Holland

Msgr. Michele Roca Cabañellas, from Spain

Msgr. Maria Paolo Krieg, from Switzerland

Msgr. Dionisio McDaid, from Ireland

Msgr. Gerardo G. Tickle, from England

Very Rev. Roberto Becker, O.M.I., from Germany

Very Rev. Vedasto Courtoisl, I.C., from France

Very Rev. Goffredo Groessel, S.V.D., from Austria

Very Rev. Giovanni Bosco Rocha, S.J., from Brasil

Very Rev. Manuel Castillo, M.Sp.S., from Mexico

Office: Piazza di Spagna, 48, Roma.
International Agency "Fides"

Very Rev. Ermanno Haeck, S.J., Director

Most Rev. Giovanni Schönhöffer, editor for German publications

Very Rev. Federico Giorgio Heinzmann, M.M., editor for English publications

Very Rev. Jesus Irigoyen, editor for Spanish publications
Very Rev. Federico Heudes, M.Sp.S., editor for French publications
Sig. Aurelio Dott. Montevecchi, editor for Italian publications
Sig. Mario Di Tullio, Clerk
Sig. Alfredo Mallucci, Clerk

Office: Via di Propaganda 1-a, Roma

GENERAL SUPERIOR COUNCIL OF THE PONTIFICAL WORK OF ST. PETER THE APOSTLE

Most Rev. Pietro Sigismondi, Titular Archbishop of Neapoli in Pisidia, Secretary of the Congregation for the Propagation of the Faith, President
Msgr. Antonio Mazza, Secretary General
Very Rev. Giacomo Pfeifer, O.M.I., Assistant of study
Sig. Edo Cav. Bonetti, Assistant of study
Sig. Carlo Rag. Scarpellini, Accountant
Sig. Franco Cav. Quagliarini, Clerk and Cashier

Consultors

The national directors of the pontifical works and in addition the following residents in Rome who belong to various nations:

Most Rev. Giovanni Battista Leone Nigris, Titular Archbishop of Filippi, from the Pontifical Society for the Propagation of the Faith
Most Rev. Faustino Tissot, S.X., Bishop of Chengchow, China (expulsed), from the Pontifical Missionary Union for the Clergy
Msgr. Amerigo Giovanelli, Substitute of the Congregation for the Oriental Church
Very Rev. Uberto D. Noots, O.Praem, Abbot General, from Belgium
Very Rev. Roberto Becker, O.M.I., from Germany
Very Rev. Romualdo Bissonnette, S.S., from Canada
Most Rev. Francesco Brennan, from U.S.A.
Msgr. Guglielmo Clapperton, from Scotland
Msgr. Guglielmo Giuseppe Leonardo Damen, from Holland
Msgr. Uberto Delatena, from Switzerland
Msgr. Carlo Duchemin, from England
Msgr. Michele Roca Cabañellas, from Spain
Msgr. Dionisio McDavid, from Ireland
Very Rev. Enrico Mauri, from Italy
Very Rev. Bosco Giovanni Rocha, S.J., from Brasil
Very Rev. Manuele Castillio, M.Sp.S., from Mexico
Very Rev. Alberto Perbal, O.M.I., from France

Office: Via di Propaganda, 1-c, Roma

GENERAL SUPERIOR COUNCIL OF THE PONTIFICAL
MISSIONARY UNION FOR THE CLERGY

Most Rev. Pietro Sigismondi, Titular Archbishop of Neapoli in Pisidia, Secretary of the Congregation for the Propagation of the Faith, President

Most Rev. Faustino Tissot, S.X., Bishop of Chengchow, China (expulsed), Secretary General

Rev. Remigio Musaragno, Assistant of the study

Consultors

The national directors of the pontifical missionary for the clergy union and in addition the following residents in Rome who belong to various nations:

Most Rev. Giovanni Battista Leone Nigris, Titular Archbishop of Filippi, from the Pontifical Society for the Propagation of the Faith

Msgr. Amerigo Giovanelli, Substitute of the Congregation for the Oriental Church

Msgr. Antonio Mazza, Secretary General of the Pontifical Association of St. Peter, the Apostle

Very Rev. Uberto D. Noots, O.Praem., Abbot General, from Belgium

Very Rev. Romualdo Bissonnette, S.S., from Canada

Very Rev. Manuel Castillo, M.Sp.S., from Mexico

Msgr. Giuseppe Guglielmo Leonardo Damen, from Holland

Msgr. Maria Paolo Krieg, from Switzerland

Very Rev. Ignazio Lee, F.S.M.I., from Latin America

Very Rev. German D. Martil, from Spain

Very Rev. Giovanni Bosco Rocha, S.J., from Brasil

Very Rev. Alberto Perbal, O.M.I., from France

Msgr. Giorgio Schwieder, from Germany

Msgr. Mariano Stroiny, from Poland

Very Rev. Giovanni Battista Tragella, from the Pontifical Institute of the Holy Apostles Peter and Paul and of Saints Ambrose and Charles for the Foreign Missions in Italy

Msgr. Giuseppe Loras Watters, from U.S.A.

Rev. Brother Alessandro Di Pietro, P.F.M.

Office: Via di Propaganda, 1-c, Roma

GENERAL SUPERIOR COUNCIL OF THE PONTIFICAL
ASSOCIATION OF THE HOLY CHILDHOOD

Protector: The Holy Father

Msgr. Adriano Bressolles, President

Most. Rev. Riccardo Ackerman, Titular Bishop of Lares, Honorary Vice-President

Msgr. Pietro Ercole, Director in Italy, Vice-President

Very Rev. Francesco Can. co D. Steels, Director in Belgium, Vice-President

Very Rev. Enrico Becquart S.M.A., Secretary

Very Rev. Giovanni Letourneur, M.Sp.S., Treasurer

Consultors: The principal national directors of the work and the representatives of other missionary institutes and the catholic lay committee which have the special missionary and administrative competence.

Financial committee: for the surveillance of deposits, the administration and also conveyance to the missions of the funds which belong to the work:

Sig. Carlo Roth-le-Gentil   Sig. Giorgio Lewandowski
                    Sig. Domenico de Grieges

Juridical Committee:

Sig. Enrico Hebrardi   Sig. Pietro Chevrier
Sig. Stefano Pruvost   Sig. Giuseppe Hamel

Office: 12 Boulevard Flandrin, 12, Paris (XVI°)

BIBLIOGRAPHY

SOURCES

Acta Apostolicae Sedis, Commentarium Officiale, Romae, 1909-1929; Civitate Vaticana, 1929-

Acta, Decreta, Normae et Vota Primi Concilii Sinensis (1924), Zi-Ka-Wei, 1929.

Acta et Decreta Sacrorum Conciliorum Recentiorum, Collectio Lacensis, 7 vols., Friburgi Brisgoviae, 1870-1892.

Acta Sanctae Sedis, 41 vols., Romae, 1865-1908.

Annuario Pontificio, Roma, *Notizie*, 1716-1861; *Annuario Pontificio*, 1862-1871; *La Gerarchia Cattolica*, 1872-1911; *Annuario Pontificio*, 1912-

Bizzarri, A., *Collectanea in Usum Secretariae Sacrae Congregationis Episcoporum et Regularium*, 2. ed., Romae, 1885.

Bouscaren, T. Lincoln, *The Canon Law Digest*, 4 vols., Milwaukee: Bruce, 1934-1958.

Bullarii Romani Continuatio Summorum Pontificum Benedicti XIV, Clementis XIII, Clementis XIV, Pii VI, Pii VII, Leonis XII et Pii VIII, 14 vols., Prati, 1840-1856.

Bullarium Diplomatum et Privilegiorum Sanctorum Romanorum Pontificum Taurinensis Editio, 24 vols, and appendix, Augustae Taurinorum-Neapoli, 1857-1872.

Bullarium Patronatus Portugalliae Regum in Ecclesiis Africae, Asiae atque Oceaniae. 6 toms. and appendix, Olisipone, 1866-1876.

Bullarium Pontificum Sacrae Congregationis de Propaganda Fide, 5 vols. and appendices, Romae, 1839-1841.

Codex Iuris Canonici, Pii X Pontificis Maximi Iussu Digestus, Benedicti XV Auctoritate Promulgatus.

Codicis Iuris Canonici Fontes, 9 vols., Vols. I-VI, ed. cura Eṁi Petri Card. Gasparri, Romae (postea Civitate Vaticana): Typis Polyglottis Vaticanis, 1923-1939. Vols. VII-IX, ed. cura et studio Eṁi Iustiniani Card. Serédi.

Collectanea S. Congregationis de Propaganda Fide, 1. ed., 2 vols., Romae: Typographia Polyglotta S.C. de Propaganda Fide, 1893; 2. ed., 2 vols., Romae, 1907.

Collection Lacensis—Acta et Decreta Sacrorum Conciliorum Recentiorum, 7 vols., Friburgi-Brisgoviae, 1870-1890.

Corpus Iuris Canonici, ed. Lipsiensis II, post Aemilii Ludovici Richteri curas instruxit Aemilius Friedberg, 2 vols., Lipsiae, 1879-1881.

De Martinis, Raphael, *Ius Pontificium de Propaganda Fide*, Prima pars, 7 vols., Romae, 1888-1894; secunda pars, 1 vol., Romae, 1909.

Denzinger, Henricus-Bannwart, Clemens-Umberg, Ioannes-Rahner, Carolus, *Enchiridion Symbolorum, Definitionum et Declarationum de Rebus Fidei et Morum*, 30. ed., Friburgi Brisgoviae: Herder, 1955.

Gardellini, Aloisius, *Decreta Authentica Congregationis Rituum ex Actis eiusdem Collecta*, 2. ed., 7 vols., Romae, 1824-1826; 3. ed., 4 vols., 1856-1858; Vol. V, 1888.

Hardouin, Jean, *Acta Conciliorum et Epistolae Decretales ac Constitutiones Summorum Pontificum*, 12 vols., Parisiis, 1714-1715.

Jaffé, Philippus, *Regesta Pontificum Romanorum* ab condita Ecclesia ad annum post Christum natum MCXCVIII, 2. ed., Correctam et auctam auspiciis Gulielmi Wattenbach, curaverunt S. Lowenfeld, F. Kaltenbrunner, P. Ewald, 2 vols., Lipsiae, 1885-1888.

Magnum Bullarium Romanum, seu eiusdem Continuatio, 19 vols. in 18, Luxemburgi, 1727-1754.

Mansi, Ioannes, *Sacrorum Conciliorum Nova et Amplissima Collectio*, 53 vols. in 60, Parisiis, 1901-1927.

Migne, Jacques Paul, *Patrologiae Cursus Completus, Series Graeca*, 161 vols., Parisiis, 1857-1866.

——, *Patrologiae Cursus Completus, Series Latina*, 221 vols., Parisiis, 1844-1855.

Potthast, Augustus, *Regesta Pontificum Romanorum* inde ab anno post Christum natum MCXCVIII ad annum MCCCIV, 2 vols., Berolini, 1874-1875.

Sacrae Romanae Decisiones seu Sententiae (ab anno 1909), Romae: Typis Vaticanis, 1912-

Sylloge Praecipuorum Documentorum Recentium Summorum Pontificum et S. Congregationis de Propaganda Fide, Romae: Typis Polyglottis Vaticanis, 1939.

Reference Works

Abbo, John A.-Hannan, Jerome D., *The Sacred Canons*, 2 vols., St. Louis: Herder, 1957.

Allgeier, Joseph L., *Canonical Obligation of Preaching in Parish Churches*, The Catholic University of America Canon Law Studies, n. 291, Washington, D. C.: The Catholic University of America Press, 1950.

Atlas Missionum a Sacra Congregatione de Propaganda Fide Dependentium cura editus eiusdem Sacrae Congregationis studio autem P. Henrici Emmerich, Vatican City, 1958.

Baart, Peter A., *The Roman Court*, 2. ed., New York, 1895.

Bargilliat, M., *Praelectiones Iuris Canonici*, 22. ed., 2 vols., Parisiis, 1905.

Bender, Ludovicus, *Potestas Ordinaria et Delegata, Commentarius in Canones 196-206*, Tournai: Desclée, 1957.

Benedictus XIV (Prospero Lambertini), *De Synodo Dioecesana*, 2. ed., 2 vols., Romae, 1806.

Benko, Matthew A., *The Abbot Nullius*, The Catholic University of

America Canon Law Studies, n. 173. Washington, D. C.: The Catholic University of America Press, 1943.

Beste, Udalricus, *Introductio in Codicem*, Collegeville, Minn.: St. John's Abbey Press, 1946.

Blat, Albertus, *Commentarium Textus Codicis Iuris Canonici*, 5 vols. in 6. Romae, 1919-1927.

Bouix, Marie Dominique, *Tractatus de Curia Romana*, Parisiis, 1859.

————, *De Concilio Provinciali*, 3. ed., Parisiis, 1884.

Bouscaren, T. Lincoln–Ellis, Adam C., *Canon Law, A Text and Commentary*, Milwaukee: Bruce, 1957.

Cance, Adrien, *Le Codé de Droit Canonique*, 7. ed., 3 vols., Paris: Gabalda, 1946.

Cappello, Felix M., *De Curia Romana* iuxta Reformationem a Pio X Sapientissime Inductam, 2 vols., Romae, 1911-1912.

————, *Summa Iuris Canonici* in Usum Scholarum Concinnata, 3 vols., Vol. I, 4. ed., Romae: Apud Aedes Universitatis Gregorianae, 1945.

Caron, Raymundus, *Apostolatus Evangelicus Missionariorum Regularium per Universum Mundum Expositus*, Antverpiae, 1653.

Champagne, Joseph E., *Manual of Missionary Action*, Trans. by Roy L. Laberge. Ottawa: University of Ottawa, 1948.

Cicognani, Amleto G., *Canon Law*, 2. ed., Reprint; Westminster, Maryland: Newman, 1949.

Chelodi, Ioannes, *Ius de Personis iuxta Codicem Iuris Canonici*, 2. ed. Tridenti, 1927.

Colomiatti, D. Emanuele, *Codex Iuris Pontificii seu Canonici*, 3 vols. in 4, Taurini, 1888.

Coronata, Matthaeus Conte a, *Institutiones Iuris Canonici*, 5 vols., Vol. I, 4. ed., 1949; Vol. II, 3. ed., 1947; Vols. III, IV, 3. ed., 1948. Taurini: Marietti.

Craisson, D., *Manuale Iuris Canonici*, 5. ed., 3 vols., Pictavii, 1877.

De Luca, Ioannes, *Theatrum Veritatis et Iustitiae sive Decisivi Discursus*, 16 vols. in 9, Coloniae, 1706.

De Meester, Alphonsus, *Iuris Canonici et Iuris Canonico-civilis Compendium*, 9. ed., 3 vols. in 4, Brugis, 1921-1928.

Dictionnaire de Droit Canonique, Paris: Leteuzey et Ané, 1924–

Documents sur l'activité missionnaire de S.S. Pie XI, Grands Lacs, Namur, 1937.

Donnelly, Francis B., *The Diocesan Synod*, The Catholic University of America Canon Law Studies, n. 74, Washington, D. C.: The Catholic University of America, 1932.

Dziob, Michael W., *The Sacred Congregation for the Oriental Church*, The Catholic University of America Canon Law Studies, n. 214, Washington, D. C.: The Catholic University of America Press, 1945.

Eubel, Conradus, *Hierarchia Catholica Medii Aevi sive Summorum Pontificum, S.R.E. Cardinalium, Ecclesiarum Antistitum Series*, 4 vols., Vols. I (1913) and II (1914) in 2. ed. edited by Gulielmus Van

Gulik-Conradus Eubel, Vol. IV (1935) edited by Patritius Gauchat under the title of *Hierarchia Catholica Medii et Recensioris Aevi sive Summorum Pontificum, S.R.E. Cardinalium, Ecclesiarum Antistitum Series,* Monasterii: Sumptibus et Typis Librariae Regensburgianae.

Fagnanus, P., *Commentaria in Quinque Libros Decretalium,* 5 vols. in 3. Coloniae, 1759.

Ferreres, Ioannes, *La Curia Romana,* Madrid, 1911.

Funk, Francis X., *History of the Church,* 2 vols., London, 1931.

Gérin, Marcel, *Le Gouvernement des Missions,* les Thèses Canoniques de Laval, n. 1, Québec: Faculté de Droit Canonique, Université Laval, 1944.

Goyau, George V., *Missions and Missionaries,* Trans. by F. M. Dreves, London, 1932.

Grentrup, Theodore, *Ius Missionarium,* Tomus I, Steyl Holland, 1925.

Guide des Missions Catholiques (Italian edition: *Guida delle Missioni Cattoliche.* Roma, 1934), 3 tom., Paris, 1936-1937.

Haine, Antoine. J.J.F., *De la Cour Romaine,* 2 vols. in 1, Louvain, 1859-1861.

Hays-Baldwin-Cole, *History of Europe,* New York: Macmillan, 1955.

Heimbucher, Max., *Die Orden und Kongregationen der katholischen Kirche,* 3. ed., 2 vols., Paderborn, 1933-1934.

Heston, Edward L., *The Holy See at Work,* Milwaukee: Bruce, 1950.

Hickey, Edward John, *The Society for the Propagation of the Faith, Its Foundation, Organization and Success* (1822-1922), The Catholic University of America Studies in American Church History, Vol. III, Washington, D. C.: The Catholic University of America Press, 1922.

Hilling, Nicholas, *Procedure at the Roman Curia,* New York, 1907.

Kubelbeck, William, *The Sacred Penitentiaria and Its Relations to Faculties of Ordinaries and Priests,* The Catholic University of America Canon Law Studies, n. 5, Washington, D. C.: The Catholic University of America, 1918.

Latourette, Kenneth Scott, *A History of Christian Missions in China,* New York: Macmillan, 1929.

Lega, Michael, *Praelectiones in Textum Iuris Canonici de Iudiciis Ecclesiasticis,* 4 vols., Romae, 1896-1901. Vols. III-IV revised in I, *De Delictis et Poenis,* Romae, 1910.

Leitner, Martinus, *De Curia Romana,* Ratisbonae, 1909.

Lemmens, Leonardus, *Acta S. Congregationis de Propaganda Fide pro Terra Sancta, Biblioteca Bio-Bibliografica della Terra Sancta e dell' Oriente Francescano,* 14 vols., 1921-1936.

Lynskey, Elizabeth M., *The Government of the Catholic Church,* New York: Kennedy and Sons, 1952.

Markham, James. J., *The Sacred Congregation of Seminaries and Universities of Studies,* The Catholic University of America Canon Law Studies, n. 384, Washington, D. C.: The Catholic University of America Press, 1957.

Maroto, Philippus, *Institutiones Iuris Canonici ad Normam Novi Codicis,* 2 vols., Vol. I, 3. ed., Romae, 1921.

Martin, Michael, *The Roman Curia,* New York, 1913.

Martin, Victor, *Les Congrégations Romaines,* Paris, 1930.

Masarei, Seraphino, *De Missionum Institutione ac de Religionibus inter Superiores Missionum et Superiores Religiosos,* Romae: Apud Universitatis Gregorianae, 1940.

McDevit, Gilbert J., *Legitimacy and Legitimation,* The Catholic University of America Canon Law Studies, n. 138, Washington, D. C.: The Catholic University of America Press, 1941.

McManus, Frederick R., *The Congregation of Sacred Rites,* The Catholic University of America Canon Law Studies, n. 352, Washington, D. C.: The Catholic University of America Press, 1954.

McSorley, Joseph, *An Outline History of the Church,* St. Louis: Herder, 1957.

Meehen, Andreas, *Compendium Iuris Canonici,* Roffae, 1899.

Meyer, Otto, *Die Propaganda, ihre Provinzen und ihre Recht,* 2 vols., Gottingen, 1852-1853.

Michiels, Gommarus, *Normae Generales Iuris Canonici,* 2. ed., 2 vols., Parisiis: Desclée, 1949.

Monin, Arthur, *De Curia Romana,* Louvanii, 1912.

Moroni, Cavaliere Gaetano, *Dizionario di Erudizione Storico-Ecclesiastica,* 103 vols., Venezia, 1840-1861.

Murphy, Francis J., *Legislative Power of the Provincial Council,* The Catholic University of America Canon Law Studies, n. 257, Washington, D. C.: The Catholic University of America Press, 1947.

Niccolò, del Re, *La Curia Romana,* Roma: Edizioni di Storia e Letteratura, 1952.

Nugent, John G., *Ordination in Societies of the Common Life,* The Catholic University of America Canon Law Studies, n. 341, Washington, D. C.: The Catholic University of America Press, 1958.

Ojetti, Benedictus, *De Romana Curia,* Romae, 1910.

———, *Synopsis Rerum Moralium et Iuris Pontificii,* Romae, 1899.

Olarte, Poblete, Elias, *The Plenary Council,* The Catholic University of America Canon Law Studies, n. 372, Washington, D. C.: The Catholic University of America Press, 1958.

Orsenigo, D., *Life of St. Charles Borromeo,* St. Louis: Herder, 1945.

Ottaviani, Alaphridus, *Institutiones Iuris Publici Ecclesiastici,* 2. ed., 2 vols., Civitate Vaticana, 1935-1936.

Pastor, Ludwig, *The History of the Popes,* 34 vols., Vols. I-IV edited by Frederick Ignatius Antrobus, Vols. VII-XXIV edited by Ralph Francis Keer, Vols. XXV-XXXIV edited by Dom Ernest Graf, St. Louis: Herder, 1898-1941.

Paventi, Xaverius, *Breviarium Iuris Missionalis,* Romae: Officium Libri Catholici, 1952.

————, *De Iuramento ac de Titulo Missionis*, Romae: Officium Libri Catholici, 1946.

————, *Organización del Instituto Español del S. Francisco Javier para Missiones Extranjeras, Commentario y Exposición de las Constitutiones*, Burgos: Aldecoa, 1950.

Payen, Gustavus, *De Matrimonio in Missionibus ac Potissimum in Sinis Tractatus Practicus et Casus*, 2. ed., 3 vols., Zi-Ka-Wei, 1935-1936.

Petra, Vincentius, *Commentaria ad Constitutiones Apostolicas*, 5 tomi, Venetiis, 1729.

Pieper, Karl, *Die Propaganda, ihre Entschehung und religiose Bedeutung*, Aix-la-Chapelle, 1922.

Prümmer, Dominicus, *Manuale Iuris Canonici*, 3. ed., Friburgi Brisgoviae, 1922.

Regatillo, Eduardus F., *Institutiones Iuris Canonici*, 4. ed., 2 vols., Santander: Sal Terrae, 1951.

Reiffenstül, Anacletus, *Ius Canonicum Universum*, 5 vols. in 7, Parisiis, 1864-1870.

Reilly, Edward M., *The General Norms of Dispensation*, The Catholic University of America Canon Law Studies, n. 119, Washington, D. C.: The Catholic University of America Press, 1939.

Sagmüller, Ioannes B., *Lehrbuch des katholischen Kirchenrechts*, 4 ed., 1 Band in 4 Teile, Freiburg in Breisgau, Teil I, 1925; Teil III, 1930; Teil IV, IV, 1934.

Sartori, Cosmas, *Iuris Missionarii Elementa*, Romae: Secretaria Missionum, O.F.M., 1947.

Schäfer, Timotheus, *De Religiosis ad Normam Codicis Iuris Canonici*, 3. ed., Romae: S.A.L.E.R., 1940.

Scherer, Rudolf Ritter, *Handbuch des Kirchenrechtes*, 2 vols., Graz-Leipzig, 1886-1898.

Schmalzgrüber, Franciscus, *Ius Ecclesiasticum Universum*, 5 vols. in 12, Romae, 1843-1845.

Schmidlin, Joseph, *Catholic Mission History*, Trans. by Matthias Braun, Techny, Ill.: Mission Press, 1933.

————, *Catholic Mission Theory*, Trans. by Matthias Braun, Techny, Ill.: Mission Press, 1931.

Sebastianelli, Guilelmus, *Praelectiones Iuris Canonici*, 3 vols., Romae, 1905-1906.

Seumois, André V., *Introduction àla Missiologie*, Schöneck-Beckenreid, Suisse: Administration der neuen Zeitscrift für Missionswissenschaft, 1952.

Simier, Iules, *La Curie Romaine*, Paris, 1906.

Sipos, Stephanus, *Enchiridion Iuris Canonici*, 2. ed., Pécs: Haladas, R.T., 1936.

Smith, S. B., *Elements of Ecclesiastical Law*, 3 vols., New York, 1877-1888.

Stanghetti, Giuseppe, *Prassi della S.C. de Propaganda Fide*, Romae: Officium Libri Catholici, 1943.

Stanton, William A., *De Societatibus sive Virirum sive Mulierum in Communi Viventium sine Votis*, 2. ed., Halifaxiae, 1936.

Toso, Albertus, *Ad Codicem Iuris Canonici Commentaria Minora*, 5 vols. in 2, Tiberini, 1921-1927.

Trede, Theodore, *Die Propaganda Fide in Rome, ihre Geschichte und ihre Bedeutung*, Berline, 1884.

Van Hove, Alphonse, *Commentarium Lovaniense in Codicem Iuris Canonici*, Vol. I, *Prolegomena*, 2. ed., Mechliniae, Romae: H. Dessain, 1945; Vol. II, *De Legibus Ecclesiasticis*, Mechliniae: H. Dessain, 1930; Vol. III, *De Temporis Supputatione*, Mechliniae: H. Dessain, 1933; Vol. IV, *De Rescriptis*, Mechliniae: H. Dessain, 1936.

Vermeersch, A.-Creusen, J., *Epitome Iuris Canonici*, 3 vols., Vol. I, 7. ed., 1949; Vol. III, 5. ed., 1936, Mechliniae-Romae: Dessain.

Vromant, Gustavus, *Ius Missionariorum de Personis*, Louvain, 1935.

————, *Ius Missionariorum—Introductio et Normae Generales*, Louvain, 1934.

————, *Ius Missionarium, De Matrimonio*, 3. ed., Paris: Desclée et Brouwer, 1947.

————, *De Fidelium Associationibus*, Louvain, 1932.

Walsh, William T., *Phillip II*, New York, 1937.

Wernz, Franciscus X., *Ius Decretalium*, 6 vols., Romae, 1898-1914; Vol. II, 3. ed., Prati, 1915.

Wernz, Franciscus, and Vidal, Petrus, *Ius Canonicum ad Codicis Normam Exactam*, 7 vols. in 8; Vol. I, 1938; Vol. II, 3. ed., a P. Philippo Aguirre recognita, 1943; Vol. V, 3. ed., a P. Philippo Aguire recognita, 1946; Vol. VI, 2. ed., a P. F. Cappello recognita, 1949, Romae: Apud Aedes Universitatis Gregorianae.

Winslow, Francis J., *Vicars and Prefects Apostolic*, The Catholic University of America Canon Law Studies, n. 24, Washington, D. C.: The Catholic University of America, 1924.

Woywod, Stanislaus, *A Practical Commentary on the Code of Canon Law*, Revised by Callistus Smith, New York: Joseph F. Wagner, 1957.

ARTICLES

Anonymous, "Des Congregations Romaines et de Leur Partique," *Analecta Iuris Pontificii*, II (1857), 2230-2283; 2364-2424.

Benigni, U., "Sacred Congregation of Propaganda," *The Catholic Encyclopedia*, XII (1911), 456-461.

Bertini, Ugo, "S.C. di Propaganda Fide," *Enciclopedia Cattolica*, IV (1950), 328-330.

Castelucci, Antonio, "Il risveglio dell' Attivita missionaria e le prime origini della S.C. de Propaganda Fide," *Le Conferenze al Laterano* (1924), pp. 117-222.

Forget, J., "Congregations Romaines," *Dictionnaires de Theologie Catholique*, III (1931), 1103-1119.

Goyau, George, "Les Initiatives Belges dans la Fondation de la Propaganda," *La Revue General,* CXII (1924), 1-23.

Grentrup, Theodore, "Die Definition des Missionbegriffes," *Zeitschrift für Missionswissenschaft,* III (1913-1914), 265-274.

———, "Die rechtlichen Beziehungen der Missionsländer zur röminschen Kurie in der Gegenwart," *Archiv für katholischens Kirchenrechts,* VCIII (1913), 147-158.

Guildey, Peter, "The Sacred Congregation de Propaganda Fide (1622-1922)," *The Catholic Historical Review,* VI (1921), 478-494.

Hilger, Joseph, "Sodality," *The Catholic Encyclopedia,* XIV (1912), 120-129.

Hilling, Nicholas, "Die rechtliche Stellung der Propagandakongregation nach der neuen Kurialreform Pius X," *Zeitschrift für Missionswissenschaft,* I (1911), 147-158.

Larraona, "Commentarium Codicis," *CpRM,* V (1924), 423.

Lega, M., "De Sacra Congregatione Christiano Nomini Propagando Praeposita, Vocari Solita 'De Propaganda Fide,'" *Annalecta Ecclesiastica,* VI (1898), 175-180; 218-223.

Magnin, "Congregation des Affairs ecclesiastiques extraordinaires," *Dictionnaire de Droit Canonique,* I (1901), 546.

Maroto, Philippus, "Studia in Constitutione Apost. Deus Scientiarum Dominus," *Apollinaris,* IV (1931), 277.

Martin, Michael, "The Roman Curia," *The Ecclesiastical Review,* XLII (1910), 541-547.

Schmidlin, Joseph, "Die Gründung der Propagandakongregation (1622)," *Zeitschrift für Missionswissenschaft,* XII (1921), 1-14.

———, "Eine Vorlauferin der Propaganda unter Klement VIII," *Zeitschrift für Missionwissenschaft,* XI (1921), 232-234.

Schmidt, John R., "The Juridic Value of the Instruction," *The Jurist,* I (1941), 289-316.

Staff, D., "De Sacrae Congregationis pro Ecclesia Orientali Competentia," *Apollinaris,* XI (1938), 358-376.

Streit, Robert, "Missionsgedanke in seiner neuzeitlichen Entwiklung," *Zeitschrift für Missionswissenschaft,* VII (1917), 1-20.

Testore, Celestino, "Agenzia Internationale Fides," *Enciclopedia Cattolica,* I (1948), 447-448.

Trede, Theodore, "Die Propaganda, ihre Entschehung und religiöse Bedeutung," *Deutsche Zeit und Streit-Fragen,* XIII (1884), V. 13.

Villian, A., "La S. Congregation de la Propaganda," *The Canoniste Contemporaine,* XXXVI (1913), 506-514.

Wojnar, Meletius M., "The Code of Oriental Canon Law, De Ritibus Orientalibus and De Personis," *The Jurist,* XIX (1959), 212-464.

Periodicals

Acta Cooperationis Missionariae Sanctae Sedis, Romae, 1938-
Acta Pontificii Operis a Propaganda Fide, Romae, 1923-1929,

Acta Pontificalium Operum a Propagatione Fidei et a Sancto Petro Apostolo pro Clero Indigena, Commentarium Officiale, Romae, 1930-

Africanae Fraternae Ephemerides Romanae, Romae, 1932-

Agence Fides (weekly publication for the correspondent missionaries, edited in five languages: French, Italian, English, Spanish, German), Romae, 1928-

Analecta Iuris Pontificii, Romae, 1855-1868; Parisiis, 1869-1890; Analecta Ecclesiastica, 1893-1911.

American Ecclesiastical Review, The (from July, 1905 to December, 1943, *The Ecclesiastical Review*), Philadelphia, 1889-1943; Washington, D. C., 1944-

Archiv für katholisches Kirchenrecht, Innsbruck, 1857-1861; Mainz, 1862-

Canoniste Contemporain, Le, Paris, 1878-1922; *Le Canoniste*, 1924-1926.

Commentarium pro Religiosis et Missionariis (from 1920 to 1934, *Commentarium pro Religiosis*), Romae, 1935-

Etudes Missionaires, Paris, 1933-

Euntes Docete, Romae, 1948-

Il Monitore Ecclesiastico, Romae, 1876-

Irish Ecclesiastical Record, The, Dublin, 1864-

Ius Pontificium, Romae, 1921-1940.

Jurist, The, Washington, D. C., 1941-

La Documentation Catholique, Paris, 1919-

Laboramus pro Missionibus, Romae, 1934-

Missionswissenschaft und Religionswissenschaft, Münster, 1938-

Monitor Ecclesiasticus, Romae, 1949-

Nouvelle Revue Thélogique, 1869-

Observatore Romano, Città del Vaticano, Sept. 5, 1849-May 27, 1852; July 1, 1861-

Periodica de Re Morali, Canonica, Liturgica (from 1905 to 1919, *De Religiosis et Missionariis Supplementum et Monumenta Periodica*; from 1921 to 1927, *Periodica de Re Canonica et Morali utilia praesertim Religiosis et Missionariis*), Brugis et Romae, 1905-1936; Romae, 1937-

Revue d'Histoire des Missions, Paris, 1924-

Zeitschrift für Missionswissenschrift und Religionswissenschaft, Münster, 1911-1922.

ABBREVIATIONS

Acta	—Lemmens, *Acta S. Congregationis de Propaganda Fide pro Terra Sancta, Biblioteca Bio-Bibliografica della Terra Sancta e dell' Oriente Francescano.*
AAS	—*Acta Apostolicae Sedis.*
ASS	—*Acta Sanctae Sedis.*
Bull. S.C.P.F.	—*Bullarium Sacrae Congregationis de Propaganda Fide.*
Bull. Rom.	—*Bullarium Diplomatum et Privilegiorum Romanorum Pontificum Taurinensis Editio.*
Coll. S.C.P.F.	—*Collectanea Sacrae Congregationis de Propaganda Fide.*
CpRM.	—*Commentarium pro Religiosis et Missionariis.*
Digest	—T. Lincoln Bouscaren, *The Canon Law Digest.*
Dizionario	—Moroni, *Dizionario di Erudizione Storico-Ecclesiastica.*
Fontes	—*Codicis Iuris Canonici Fontes.*
Guida	—*Guida delle missioni cattoliche Redacta sotto gli auspici della Sacra Congregatione de Prop. Fide.*
Hierarchia	—*Hierarchia Catholica Medii Aevi sive Summorum Pontificum, S.R.E. Cardinalium, Ecclesiarum Antistitum Series.*
Mansi	—Mansi, *Sacrorum Conciliorum Nova et Amplissima Collectio.*
Normae Communes	—*Ordo Servandus in Sacris Congregationibus, Tribunalibus, Officii Romanae Curiae, Pars Prima, Normae Communes.*
Normae Peculiares	—*Ordo Servandus . . . . Pars Altera, Normae Peculiares.*
Prassi	—Stanghetti, *Prassi della S.C. de Propaganda Fide.*
Sylloge	—*Sylloge Praecipuorum Documentorum Recentium Summorum Pontificum et S. Congregationis de Propaganda Fide.*
S.C.S. Off.	—*Sacra Congregatio Sancti Officii.*
S.C. Consist.	—*Sacra Congregatio Consistorialis.*
S.C. Sacr.	—*Sacra Congregatio Sacramentorum.*
S.C. Rel.	—*Sacra Congregatio Religiosorum.*
S.C.P.F.	—*Sacra Congregatio de Propaganda Fide.*
S.C. Orient.	—*Sacra Congregatio pro Ecclesia Orientali.*

INDEX

BIOGRAPHICAL NOTE

Raphael Hung Sik Song was born in Kang-Won, Do, Korea, on November 15, 1926. In April, 1941, he was admitted to St. Willibrord's Seminary in Tok-Won, Ham-Keng-Nam, Do. From 1949 to 1951, he studied at the University of Fribourg in Fribourg, Switzerland. In the spring of 1951, he entered the College of the Holy Ghost (Major Seminary), Seoul. On June 24, 1954, he was ordained to the priesthood at the Pro-Cathedral in Taegu.

His first assignment after ordination was to Pusan-Jin Church, Pusan, where he remained until July, 1956, when he was appointed Secretary of the Vicariate Apostolic of Taegu. In January, 1957, he was sent to Seton Hall University, South Orange, New Jersey, where he received the degree of Master of Arts in June, 1958. In September, 1958, he was enrolled in the School of Canon Law of the Catholic University of America, where he received the degree of Bachelor of Canon Law in June, 1959, and the degree of Licentiate in Canon Law in June, 1960.

CANON LAW STUDIES *

416. Cunningham, Rev. Thomas M., O.S.M., J.C.L., The Canonical Suppression of Religious Houses.
417. McGough, Rev. James P., J.C.L., The Laws of the State of Mississippi Affecting Church Property.
418. Nace, Rev. Arthur J., A.B., M.A., J.C.L., The Right to Accuse a Marriage of Invalidity.
419. Renati, Rev. Charles G., A.B., J.C.L., The Recipient of Extreme Unction.
420. Song, Rev. Raphael H., M.A., J.C.L., The Sacred Congregation for the Propagation of the Faith.

* For a complete list of the available numbers of this series apply to the Catholic University of America Press, 620 Michigan Avenue, N.E., Washington (17), D. C., for a general catalogue.

9 780813 225777